Engaging in the Leadership Process

Identity, Capacity, and Efficacy for College Students

A Volume in Contemporary Perspectives on Leadership Learning

Series Editor

Kathy L. Guthrie
Florida State University

Engaging in the Leadership Process

Identity, Capacity, and Efficacy for College Students

by

Kathy L. Guthrie

Cameron C. Beatty

and

Erica R. Wiborg

INFORMATION AGE PUBLISHING, INC.
Charlotte, NC • www.infoagepub.com

Library of Congress Cataloging-in-Publication Data

CIP record for this book is available from the Library of Congress
http://www.loc.gov

ISBNs: 978-1-64802-465-8 (Paperback)

         978-1-64802-466-5 (Hardcover)

         978-1-64802-467-2 (ebook)

CONTENTS

CHAPTER 1

LEADERSHIP

How Do I Engage in the Process?

What do you think of when you hear the word leadership? Do certain people come to mind? Did you think of a business leader, like Elon Musk or Sheryl Sandberg? Or did a politician come to mind, like Barack Obama or John McCain? Or a sports figure like Megan Rapinoe or LeBron James? If a person came to mind, you actually thought of a leader. The words leadership and leader often get interchanged although they are two different concepts. The premise of this book is that anyone, whether you hold a position or not, can be a leader. Both leaders and followers engage in the process of leadership. We also believe to fully engage in leadership as a leader, individuals need to think about their identity, capacity, and efficacy as a leader. More on that later.

PURPOSE OF THIS BOOK

We are guessing that you are reading this book because you want to learn more about the process of leadership and how to be a leader. This book is about leadership learning and how we each can best develop as leaders.

Engaging in the Leadership Process:
Identity, Capacity, and Efficacy for College Students, pp. 1–16
Copyright © 2021 by Information Age Publishing

This book is relatively short and hopefully, you will be engaged from the very beginning (now) until the end. We hope it is packed full of aspects of leadership that will cause you to pause, consider, and think about how leadership shows up in your life, and how you can apply it moving forward. This first chapter takes you through the foundations of leadership and several points we believe about leadership. It will provide some definitions and how to get the most out of this book. Chapters 2–4 dig into the ideas of identity, capacity, and efficacy in leadership learning. Identity, capacity, and efficacy are our ways of understanding leadership, which is a key component of the culturally relevant leadership learning (CRLL) model (Bertrand Jones et al., 2016). We will dig into identity (who you are), capacity (your ability), and efficacy (what you do) and the CRLL model more throughout this book. In the last chapter, Chapter 5, we bring it all together and discuss our hope for the future and you as a leader. We are excited that you are going on this journey of learning with us. Now first, let's talk about this concept of leadership.

LEADERSHIP IS COMPLEX

According to scholar Barbara Kellerman (2012) there are over 1,500 definitions and 40 models of leadership. The definition of leadership has become more debated than agreed upon and definitions on leadership range from ideas rooted that only physically strong white men can be leaders (see great man theory, Carlyle, 1888) to efforts toward positive social and community change (see social change model of leadership development, Astin & Astin, 1996). As Guthrie and Jenkins (2018) point out, "Individuals may define this complex concept differently based on personal identities, experiences, traits, behaviors, or worldviews" (p. 4). In fact, several scholars have said that leadership is socially constructed and so it holds different meanings to different people (Guthrie et al., 2013). Socially constructed means that over time, our understandings of a complex idea, in this case, leadership, have been jointly created from shared assumptions. Shared assumptions have incredible influence because of the collective nature and overall cultural impacts they have. Social construction centers on the idea that meanings are developed with others rather than separately within each individual.

Historically, James MacGregor Burns (1978) created a dramatic shift in the conversation among Western leadership scholars, which moved from conceptualizing leadership from an industrial to a postindustrial framework. Industrial definitions equated leadership with a position, essentially being at the top of power hierarchies and directing others. Rost (1991) simplified industrial ideas of leadership as simply good management. Challenging the notions of one individual being a leader who single-handedly creates a vision and executes it, Burns (1978) led leadership thinking to postindustrial conceptions of leadership. These postindustrial concepts were instead rooted in mutual relationships as vital components of leadership processes. Whereas industrial frameworks of leadership focus on position, postindustrial frameworks focus on building relationships and process to collectively make change. Postindustrial concepts and models introduced a new paradigm in leadership studies; one that differentiates leader and leadership, the person, and the process. Traditional roles, as we typically know them, would fit into the industrial paradigm. For example, a president of an organization or the Chief Operating Officer of a corporation; those positions that give people the power to manage.

Although many authors have defined leadership over the years (over 1,500 ways, right?), Rost (1991) dedicated an entire book to exploring the historical evolution of the word *leadership* and the accompanying definitions. He attempted to develop a definition of leadership from analyzing how everyone else defined it. After much deliberation, Rost (1991) settled on this definition: "leadership is an influence relationship among leaders and followers who intend real change that reflects their mutual purposes" (p. 102). Rost's definition of leadership makes it operational for all engaged in the process of leadership. This includes leaders, followers, and those who want to create real change, not just for those who are in positions of power. Before we go any further, we want to share some of our foundational beliefs regarding leadership. Some of these beliefs you may or may not agree with, but we wanted to make sure we are clear in where we are coming from. These beliefs include:

- *Anyone May Engage in the Process of Leadership.* Regardless of positional power, leadership is open to everyone to participate, not just a "chosen" few. Seeing those with titles as the only people who are leaders is an extremely outdated notion. Essentially, leaders are the individuals, with or without formal positions of authority, who work collectively to tackle problems.
- *Leaders are Made: Leadership can be Learned.* Have you heard that "Leaders are born, not made?" Don't believe this for a second! The truth is most capacities and competencies of leadership can be learned. We all can learn, grow, and improve if the basic desire to develop is there.
- *Leaders are Followers Also.* Leadership is often revealed through followership. You can be both a coach and a team player. Leadership is the collaboration and interactions between leaders and followers, and the process occurring amongst and between them.

Being a leader and follower is fluid in nature. One minute you may be acting as a leader and a follower the next.

- *Leadership Shows Up Differently Depending on Context.* The process of leadership can be exhibited in many ways. This depends on the context in which leaders and followers are interacting, who these leaders and followers are, and the situation they are working with and through.
- *Leaders Do Not Have to Be the Loudest in the Room.* Extroversion and charisma are not required to be a leader. While extroverts can be more likely to network, introverts can be more introspective. Both are needed and valued in the leadership process.
- *Leadership Is Ethical.* There are many examples of people wielding power who have acted unethically. We hold the belief that to be a leader and engage in the process of leadership, you need to be ethical. Ethical leaders stand on solid principles and values and have a moral compass. They value integrity, equality, and transparency. As a leader, what values are important to you?

Language of Leadership

Language is important. Specifically, what words we use to describe something, how we phrase them, and the intent behind what we are saying are all critical to how messages are given and received. Guthrie and colleagues (2013) explained that language is not only used for communication, but it also offers insight into our individual and collective worldviews. Just as in everything we encounter, words and underlying definitions matter in the language of leadership. Oftentimes scholarship on leadership confuse leader and leadership; two words mistakenly substituted for each other with little distinction (Dugan & Komives, 2011). Careless interchanging confuses the person (leader) and the process (leadership). When used interchangeably, leadership becomes the work of one versus all. This can not only lead to confusion, but it will also most likely leave out people who never saw themselves in leadership language and the definitions provided. Essentially, assumptions of what leadership is and how we talk about it determines the ability to reach various people (Warner & Grint, 2006). These assumptions ground observations of who is considered a leader and how the process of leadership is defined. That is why it is important to think deeply about the concepts of leader, leadership, follower, followership, as well as how management is different from leadership.

We know you may have never thought about leadership and leader as different before. That is okay! It is confusing, especially when you may have been taught that leader equals a title or position. As you continue through this book and in your leadership journey, the complexity of leadership will become clearer. Stick with us. The next paragraph will hopefully provide more insight into the differences between leader and leadership

Leader and Leadership

In the simplest of terms, a leader is the individual and leadership is the process we engage in. When we focus on our development as a leader, we focus on ourselves as an individual. This might be enhancing our intra-personal growth, understanding our self, or enhancing our knowledge so we can build our human capital, which are the knowledge, skills, and experiences you possess, as a leader. When we concentrate on our leadership development, we are focusing on relationships and opportunities to understand a group and expanding the collective capacity of all involved. Leadership development builds social capital, which are the networks of relationships you have, and increases organizational value. Individual leader focus may be in a formal or informal role, but the collective leadership focus is how people can come together to do work in meaningful ways. For example, think about a student organization you may be involved in. Individuals (leaders) may hold specific responsibilities or roles, president, chair of a committee, or motivator, to keep the group moving forward. The group coming together with those individuals to engage in meaningful work collectively (leadership) is how the student organization fulfills its mission.

Follower and Followership

Essentially, a follower is an individual who engages in behaviors while interacting with leaders in an effort to make change and meet needed objectives alongside leaders. However, the role of a follower is not a simple one. Followers may work independently, be accountable for their actions, and/or take ownership of necessary tasks. Followership is best defined as an intentional practice on the part of the follower to enhance the cooperative interchange between the follower and the leader. Engaging in the process is followership, which is also another social construct that is integral to the leadership process. In enhancing followership skills, one must focus on improving necessary talents, such as accountability, self-management, and analytical thinking. Regardless of the motivation of being a follower, they see that their role is indeed essential. Good leaders not only know when they should be a follower, but they should gain a clear understanding of the role and strengths of followers in the various contexts in which they engage.

Leadership and Management

Leadership and management are two concepts that, while they share many similarities, they are very different. Kotter (1990) points out how leadership can be considered a concept that has been around for centuries, while management is an idea developed only in the last 100 years, partially from the rise of the Industrial Revolution. One thing to stress is that an individual can be both a great leader and a great manager but being a leader and a manager both require the mastery of slightly different skills. As seen Figure 1.1, Rost (1991) provides four points in which leadership and management differ in the areas of relationship, roles, changes, and overall purpose. Leadership is based on an influential relationship, where management is focused on an authoritative relationship. Leader and follower roles emerge in the process of leadership, where manager and subordinate roles exist in the management process. Leadership intends real changes, where management focuses on producing something and potentially selling a product (if you are a business). The final point Rost (1991) makes is that intended changes in leadership reflect mutual purposes where goods and services are goals that result in coordinated activities in management. Both leadership and management involve relationships, working with people, and working with effective goals and purposes. Think about where you have seen leadership and management show up in an organization you are a part of or in your classes. How do the needed skills differ?

HOW DOES ONE LEARN LEADERSHIP?

As we have been discussing, how individuals engage in this process of leadership, both as leaders and followers is complex. So, how does one learn leadership? First, it is important to understand that leadership depends on multiple perspectives from various disciplines. The study of leadership is interdisciplinary and needs to be applied to different aspects of our daily life. Also, situating how leadership shows up in the United States is essential to framing our learning leadership.

Where Does Learning Leadership Come From?

Ayman et al. (2003) state that for the past several centuries, different societies have expressed interest in developing leaders. How to be a leader or develop leadership is not a new topic- that is for sure. Some argue that teaching (and learning for that matter) evolved from the writings of the

Figure 1.1

Leadership vs. Management

Leadership vs. Management

Leadership	Management
▸ Influence Relationship	▸ Authority Relationship
▸ Leaders and Followers	▸ Managers and Subordinates
▸ Intend Real Changes	▸ Produce and Sell Goods and/or Products
▸ Intended Changes Reflect Mutual Purposes	▸ Good/Services Result from Coordinated Activities

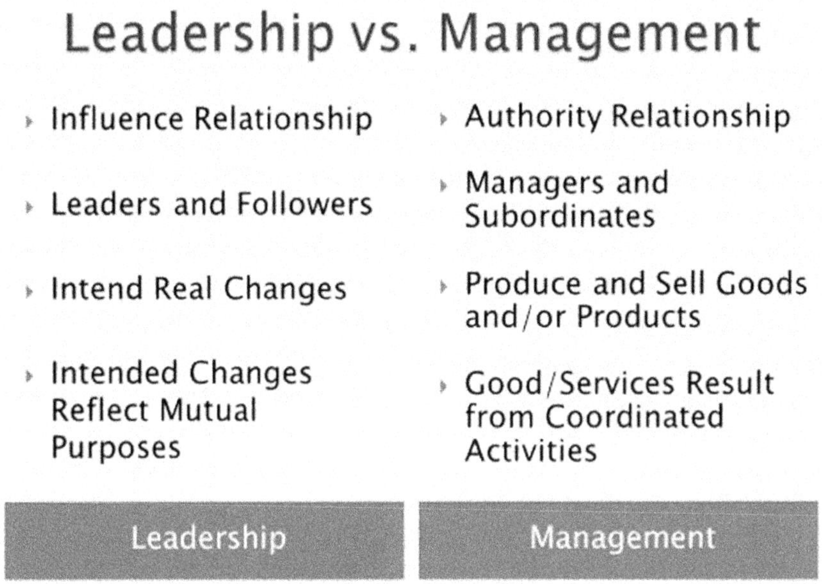

Adapted from Rost (1991). *Leadership for the Twenty-first Century.* Praeger.

ancient Greek philosophers, Plato and Aristotle (Birkelund, 2000). Plato's student, Aristotle, in *Nicomachean Ethics* wrote, "That is why we need to have had the appropriate upbringing—right from early youth, as Plato says —to make us find enjoyment or pain in the right things; for this is the correct education" (Irwin, 1999, p. 21). Burkhardt and Zimmerman-Oster (1999) discuss how Aristotle placed importance on educating future leaders. This can be seen in his teaching and mentoring of the ancient military leader and conqueror, Alexander the Great. This brief historical look at early philosophers provides a foundational context for how leadership was taught, from multiple perspectives. History also allows us to acknowledge the limitations of leadership and why it is critical to keep evolving. Studying leadership from political, linguistic, psychological, historical, cultural, and sociological perspectives enhances one's understanding of various leadership approaches (Harvey & Riggio, 2011). Not only is it important to note how multiple perspectives are important for leadership learning, but we also need to recognize how leadership has evolved in the context of the United States.

Leadership Learning in the United States

Although the concept of leadership has been discussed since Plato and Aristotle's time, the term "leadership" did not come into the English language until the late 19th century (Brungardt, 1998). At the beginning of the 20th century, leadership caught the attention of the United States government, American businesses, and higher education (Riggio et al., 2003). The first hint of leadership as a potential field of study emerged in 1940 when the United States government funded research projects in an effort to gain advantages during World War II. This was to increase efficiency and effectiveness, private enterprises funded leadership research within higher education institutions. An example of corporate involvement in promoting leadership research is the Smith Richardson Foundation, which funded research leading to one of the most influential books in the field of leadership, Stodgill's *Handbook of Leadership* (Riggio et al., 2003). Leadership learning in the United States has a significant history, but how do we learn leadership today?

Leadership Learning Framework

One way to frame how we learn leadership is to use the metaphor of a steering wheel. The leadership learning framework (Guthrie & Jenkins, 2018) provides a visual mechanism for how we all should be steering our own learning. As seen in Figure 1.2, leadership knowledge encompasses the entire wheel. Knowledge of leadership theories, concepts, and skills is foundational for all leadership learning. We can gain leadership knowledge from different sources, starting with the language we use about leadership. Looking back at the wheel, there are four aspects of development, training, observation, and engagement which all contribute to metacognition. Metacognition (thinking about your thinking) sits at the heart of leadership learning because without critical thought and reflection of the learning experience, we cannot make meaning or begin to apply and adapt what we learn. Now, let's discuss these six aspects of leadership learning in more detail. As we discuss these aspects in more depth, think about how you have learned leadership in the past and how you feel you best learn leadership now.

To learn *leadership knowledge* is to acquire information and critical insights about the process of leadership. Increasing leadership knowledge is cognitive and focuses on simply learning new concepts, constructs, and theories related to leadership. It is an essential aspect of overall leadership learning. You can learn leadership theories and concepts both in and out of the classroom, outside of the classroom could include student organizations

Figure 1.2

Leadership Learning Framework

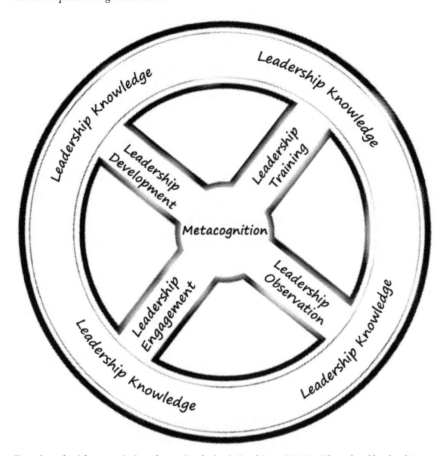

Reprinted with permission from Guthrie & Jenkins (2018). *The role of leadership educators: Transforming learning.* Information Age Publishing.

or community service work. Leadership concepts can then be applied to personal experiences, which completes a practical model and allows you to put leadership knowledge into action.

Leadership development refers to the human and intrapersonal aspects of leadership learning. This is where learning focuses on the individual and their values, needs, personal motivation, readiness to lead, identity, and multiple other dimensions of self. This aspect of leadership learning may include knowledge of and experiential exposure to ethics, consciousness of self, authenticity, citizenship, receiving feedback, engaging in reflection, healthy self-esteem, flexibility, and emotional self-regulation (Shankman et al., 2015). For example, a student organization leadership workshop could focus on developing individual self-awareness, community relationship building, and how to be ethical, which are all a part of the human and intrapersonal aspects of leadership learning.

Leadership training is central to leadership learning given its focus on the skill- and competency-based behavioral aspects of learning. This type of leadership learning places heavy emphasis on practicing and building upon previous lessons. This approach allows us to work toward mastery and observable behavioral change through development of skills and competencies. Leadership training may include meeting management, facilitation, decision making, negotiation, public speaking, listening, establishing a vision, providing feedback, and supervision.

Leadership observation refers to the social, cultural, and observational aspects of leadership learning. This type of learning is making meaning and allows learners to see how effective and ineffective leaders and followers act in relation to others in social and cultural contexts. However, in observation, the learner is a passive recipient, which leads to reflection and making meaning of what is seen. It is important to note that learning is always culturally bound (Merriam & Caffarella, 1999), which is powerful for learning what leadership looks like in different cultures. An example of observation could be noticing how an administrator facilitates a conversation with your group or noticing how an upperclassman leads the effort in planning a fundraising event. This type of learning is observing others and reflecting on how you might use parts of what you saw.

Leadership engagement refers to the experiential, relational, interactional, and interpersonal aspects of leadership learning. Like leadership observation, leadership engagement is constructed from the learner's experience. However, in leadership engagement, the learner is an active participant. Specifically, learners construct meaning in response to direct and personal encounters with the activities of leadership. Ultimately, the purpose of engagement is to enhance the development of leaders; learning from an engagement perspective through interpersonal means is effective for learners globally, not just the highly researched Western context (Krauss & Hamid, 2015). Many of you might think of this right away— actually engaging in the process. This is learning by doing. Whether it is participating in a recruitment committee or leading your group for a final presentation, this type of learning is by engaging in the process.

Leadership metacognition refers to the reflective, organizational, analytical, evaluative, adaptive, processual, mindful, and complex aspects of leadership learning. In this aspect, the learner is critically aware and understands their thoughts about the leadership process and the learning of leadership. Meichenbaum (1985) referred to metacognition as a mindfulness of one's knowledge and the ability to recognize, control, and use one's cognitive processes. This understanding includes knowing when, where, and why to use particular strategies for problem-solving and learning. Another way to think about learning by metacognition is when you have an "ah-ha" moment, one when several learning moments come together and bring awareness to the situation you are in. You may ask yourself tough questions regarding a program you are trying to plan or reflect on how you can be a better follower or leader in certain situations.

IDENTITY, CAPACITY, AND EFFICACY

Since identity, capacity, and efficacy are so important to your leadership journey, there will be opportunities to learn and reflect on what these terms mean and how they show up for you throughout this book. We will introduce the concepts to you now to get you thinking about how they connect to your personal leadership learning journey. First, let us start with identity. Just like leadership, identity is a socially constructed concept. As you can imagine, identity and other socially constructed concepts are grounded in historical, cultural, and political norms. Identity is a constantly evolving self-portrait encompassing multiple dimensions of self (Jones & Abes, 2013). When describing self, it is important to interrogate the assumptions which might ground the use of language when discussing salient social identities. For example, choices between girl and woman, Mexican or Latinx, or deaf as opposed to hearing-impaired represent differences beyond word choice. One's thoughts about who they are as a leader is their leader identity (Guthrie et al., 2013). We will explore more about social identities and leader identity in Chapter 2.

Capacity is often defined as the ability to hold, contain, or absorb something or the ability to retain knowledge. This is also true with leadership capacity. As Dugan (2017) defines capacity, it is the integration of knowledge, skills, and attitudes which lead to an overall ability to engage effectively in the leadership process. However, capacity should not be confused with potential. Leadership potential is realizing your ability to be a leader. Leadership capacity is already having the ability to be a leader, but receiving, holding, and absorbing the knowledge, skills, values, and attitude to be a leader. Essentially, your leadership potential must be realized before your leadership capacity can be enhanced.

As *Merriam-Webster* dictionary defines it, efficacy is "the ability to produce a desired result." More specifically, Bandura (1997) defined efficacy as how one can execute a plan of action towards an intended outcome. In other words, it is the belief we can be successful at specific activities. With that in mind, leadership efficacy is our belief in our ability to effectively engage in the process of leadership using our knowledge, skills, values, and attitudes we have learned. While continuing to build our capacity and our belief in ourselves, our efficacy allows for us to center our belief in executing common goals with others engaged in the leadership process. Identity, capacity, and efficacy, and the interplay of these concepts are crucial to understanding our personal leadership learning journey. However, to really dig into your leadership learning journey, better understanding of cultural relevance in leadership learning is critical.

CULTURAL RELEVANCE IN LEADERSHIP LEARNING

As just discussed, we believe identity, capacity, and efficacy are critical to our individual understanding of leadership and being a leader. We also strongly believe that cultural relevance is critical in learning leadership and is essential in developing as a leader. Bertrand Jones and colleagues (2016) developed the culturally relevant leadership learning (CRLL) model which is interwoven throughout this book. You will see the influence this model has on our thinking regarding leadership and how to best develop as a leader. So, we wanted to share a bit more about it.

CRLL considers the perspectives of students from diverse backgrounds, whether that is related to race, ethnicity, gender, social class, ability, social location, and how diverse students learn. It encourages contemplating what diverse students bring into learning spaces with their identities, capacities, and efficacies. This model also acknowledges the dynamics of oppression and power in leadership, and how they influence student leaders' ability and willingness to create social change (Bertrand Jones et al., 2016). Leader identity, capacity, and efficacy are focused on in leadership development while taking into consideration a broader organizational culture.

Five Critical Dimensions to Consider

Within organizational culture (whatever organization you might be a part of), CRLL takes into consideration five critical dimensions which include: (a) historical legacy of inclusion and exclusion, (b) compositional diversity, (c) psychological climate, (d) behavioral climate, and (e) organizational/structural aspects (Bertrand Jones et al., 2016). *Historical legacy of inclusion and exclusion* forces us to think about who has traditionally participated in your organization and how they have engaged in the leadership process. What does the history of your organization tell you? *Compositional diversity* represents the proportion of various populations who are represented in your organization, as both leaders and followers. Who shows up to engage in your organization? The ***psychological dimension*** emphasizes attitudes about difference, perceptions of discrimination, and individual views of group relations in your organization. What do individuals (both leaders and followers) think about the health of the group overall? Interactions and the quality of interaction across difference in your organization is the ***behavioral dimension***. How do people act in your organization, especially while engaging in the leadership process? Finally, the ***organizational/ structural dimension*** focuses on what processes guide the operation of your organization. What do your policies and overall structure reveal about your organization?

Environments and cultures in which we are a part of directly influence our growth, development, and learning. CRLL acknowledges how external forces influence contexts for leadership development. The intent behind the five domains of culturally relevant leadership learning is to motivate and empower each of us in our leadership learning journey to consider the importance of individual experiences, and how we engage in the leadership learning context.

JOURNEY OF LEADERSHIP LEARNING

Dedicating yourself to learn leadership is not only an investment in yourself, but also in the people you engage with. Whether it is family, friends, classmates, or fellow organizational members, learning how to be a better leader and engage in the leadership process more effectively will also make you more self-aware in all aspects of your life. We think of leadership learning as an exciting journey, one with many aspects to consider. In fact, you have been on this journey for quite some time. You have been observing, practicing, and critiquing leadership since you were in Kindergarten. Imitating parents, playing on the playground at school, or working in centers in your classroom, you have been engaging in the process of leadership and learning leadership well before you picked up this book. Hopefully, this book continues you on this journey of leadership learning and helps you think more deeply about your own leadership experiences. Using the journey metaphor, the figures on the next page helps us imagine that we are in a car driving. You have the leadership learning framework discussed above as the steering wheel, and you, as the learner bring various things to the journey. Three of these things are identity, capacity, and efficacy, which are your ways of understanding leadership. So, buckle up. Let's continue this journey together.

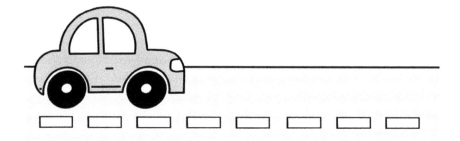

HOW TO USE THIS BOOK

Throughout this book, you will see images that will encourage you to engage with and reflect on the content in different ways. Below are brief descriptions and in some cases, questions, and activities for you to start with this first chapter.

Call-In Boxes. At the beginning of each remaining chapter you will see this symbol which is "calling" you into learning and the content of that chapter. These call-in boxes will provide you questions you should consider as you work your way through the material. These questions invite you to think about the material and how it applies to your own experiences.

Pause for Consideration. Throughout chapters there will be moments that we want you to pause and consider the information we are providing. In many cases, we will ask you to apply what we are talking about to your own experiences.

PERSONAL REFLECTION

In this section, questions will be offered for you, the reader, to personally reflect on the material presented in this chapter. Take a few minutes to consider these questions to further your leadership learning.

- Have you ever thought about how you learn leadership? Looking at the six aspects of the Leadership Learning Framework, what aspect best fits with your overall learning style?
- Think back to your earliest memory of seeing someone that you can now define as a leader. Who was that person? What made them a leader in your mind?
- Now think back to when you first identified as a leader. Did someone call you a leader specifically? Or did you realize that you influenced others in certain situations? What do these memories bring up for you?

DISCUSSION QUESTIONS

Being in dialogue with others is a good way to reflect and make meaning to enhance your leadership learning. This section will provide questions that can serve as a guide for discussing concepts with classmates, friends, or family.

Imagine you were initiating a positive change as part of an organization you are a part of. What aspects of leadership would be influential for you and other members of your organization to exhibit? Why?

It is important for leaders to also be followers; can you describe a time when you felt you were a strong follower? What qualities did you have that made you a reliable follower?

TAKING LEADERSHIP LEARNING FURTHER

Leadership learning not only involves knowledge development, reflecting, and practicing skills, but also engaging in additional activities that enhance your ability to engage in the leadership process. Each chapter will provide two activities at the end of the chapter for you to continue your leadership learning journey, broadly or specifically to your identity, capacity, or efficacy.

Activity #1: What is "Good" Leadership?

"Good" is in quotes here, because good depends on perspective. As we have already discussed, leadership is socially constructed. This means that depending on your experience, you may define "good" leadership differently than classmates and friends. To get you thinking about how you define leadership, specifically "good" leadership, think about your own leadership learning history and when you had positive leadership experiences. You can write the answers to these questions in a journal, jot them down on a piece of paper, discuss them with a friend or family member, or any other way of reflecting on what has influenced your definition of "good" leadership.

- Recall the leaders you have most admired in your life. These are the individuals who you have followed or would follow if the opportunity presented itself. What skills do they have that you respect? Do they have specific abilities you try to emulate? How did you respond to them as a follower?
- Now, remember moments when you were proud of how you engaged in leadership. What did you do specifically? What feedback did others give you in this process?
- Using both reflections about a role model and yourself, how do you define "good" leadership? How does your identity, capacity, and efficacy play a part in "good" leadership?

Activity #2: I Am. I Can. I Do.

Considering your reflection on being a leader and the process of leadership, respond to the following prompts.

I am….

I can…

I do…

As you work through the next chapters, think about how your responses to the above prompts frame your identity (I am), capacity (I can), and efficacy (I do). Reflect on how the context in which you were raised, and your experiences have socially constructed your view of leadership and how you want to intentionally continue your leadership learning journey.

CHAPTER 2

IDENTITY

Who Am I?

As we continue to explore and learn more about ourselves as leaders, we must consider who and what we understand ourselves to be and how that influences our leadership experiences. This chapter explores how you define your identities in relationship to how society has structured group membership. Through this book, we will continue to explore our own identity as a leader and how that builds capacity and efficacy for leadership. As we move through this chapter consider the following questions:

- Think about how you define yourself.
- When asked the question, "What identities do you hold?" How do you think about that question?
- What identities do you think about daily?
- How has society defined those identities and how you see yourself?
- What group memberships do you hold that help to inform (both at a personal level and a societal level) your identity?

Engaging in the Leadership Process:
Identity, Capacity, and Efficacy for College Students, pp. 17–32
Copyright © 2021 by Information Age Publishing
All rights of reproduction in any form reserved.

If you have ever seen a Disney, Marvel, or DC Comics movie, you know that each superhero's story is unique, but you also might have noticed common themes and plotlines to each hero's story. A person discovering they are special in some way because of some inherited or newly discovered super-power. This power either disrupted or contributed to how the superhero saw themselves. Many of these heroes go on a story arc to exploring who they are and where they came from. Many find out new things about their background, their family, and what role the government played in them gaining these superpowers. Their self-identity is in limbo or being (re) defined by outside norms and expectations.

Who am I? That is the question each superhero asks themselves and many people have spent a lifetime trying to answer. Our identity is often attached to our family, our ancestors, where we grew up, religious traditions, and community norms. How many times have you answered questions or engaged in small talk? These social interactions give us context of who a person is, no matter how surface level the conversation might feel. We are making connections in our mind about the person and the person is making meaning of us and our identities based on the social interaction. Identity is both personal and socially constructed. What we mean by that is, each of us have individual personalities, likes and dislikes, and personal experiences that shape how we define our identities. But we cannot ignore how in society there have been historical and political influences that have shaped group memberships—such as race, gender identity, and socioeco-nomic status—are treated. Next, we will explore group membership and social identities and how you define your personal identities.

LEADERSHIP AND LEADER IDENTITY DEFINED

We know that we are each individuals with personal values and characteristics, but how do you consider your identity in relation to group membership? Josselson stated (1996), "Identity is not just a private, individual matter [but] a complex negotiation between person and society" (p. 31). When completing any application for college or for a job, we are often asked to share our gender, race, religious affiliation, national origin, ability, and other social identities. The construction of identity happens when we start to understand the cultural contexts in which we live, interact with other people, and absorb the cultural messages that surround us (Davis & Harrison, 2014). Examples of cultural contexts were highlighted in the dimensions of the culturally relevant leadership learning model (see Chapter 1). Understanding your social identities supports how you see yourself as well as how you are perceived by others (Guthrie & Jenkins, 2018). We have no control over how others perceive us, but we can be mindful of how we perceive and pass judgments on others. When we start to consider identity as being socially constructed, we disrupt this "notion that individual hard work and character are the only forces at play in determining who succeeds and who doesn't, and who has access to vital resources and who has hurdles in the pursuit of life, liberty, and happiness" (Davis & Harrison, 2014, p. 33). When you swim with a current, you don't feel the current the same as swimming against the current and you swim faster than you would otherwise. The current can be an analogy for social privilege and if it flows with you, it simply propels you forward with little effort of your own. Our socially constructed identities contribute to how we experience society, engage in leadership, what privileges or advantages we receive, and how we make meaning of those who have different social identities.

What Are Social Identities?

Scholars have used the term social identity to describe how students made sense of their race, class, gender, sexuality, and other forms of identity as aspects of the self that exist within a social context. Social identities are understood to influence your relationship with others and how you are perceived in comparison to societal norms (McEwen, 2003). However, according to Ruderman and Ernst (2004), the original definition of social identity, by Henry Tajfel, described it as both the knowledge of belonging to a certain group and that belonging has a value or significance to the person in some way. The term social identity also refers to social categories or constructed social groups (Stryker & Burke, 2000). Additionally, the meaning of social identity refers to "an overall sense of self or sense of being" (McEwen, 2003, p. 205). Understanding one's social identities is the social construction of self and how one defines self is based on social spaces and our socialization in these spaces.

Socialization is the process by which we learn about our culture, the culture of others and how to live within the norms of our society (Davis & Harrison, 2013). Socialization allows for us to learn how to perceive our world. Understanding our own identities and exploring how to engage with others is also important to socialization. Socialization and understanding others applies to those who hold different and similar social identities to our own. This socialization process happens in different public institutions in society, like schools, places of employment, religious institutions, media, and our own family. Socialization does not just happen early in our lives but can extend into adulthood as we have new transitions in our lives or take on new identities. Harro (2000) is a social justice scholar who shared well cited descriptions of both the cycle of socialization and the cycle of liberation (see Chapter 5); he described the cycle of socialization as the process of how we are socialized into a specific identity. The process entails first being born into the world with our identities chosen, then socialization on a personal level, and then how those identities are reinforced by society and larger systems. This socialization happens both in how we think about ourselves, and how we relate to others. For example, we are told messages for our gender like, boys don't cry or girls should stay in their place. These messages then contribute to gender roles and norms at the institution level, at places like school and church. Finally, these messages are reinforced through society and cultural norms like music, media, films, and fashion.

Model of Multiple Dimensions of Identity (MMDI)

The Model of Multiple Dimensions of Identity (MMDI) represents multiple social identities as intersecting (see Figure 2.1). Identities are not distinct separate identities from one another, but they are connected and ever changing as a person evolves in various contexts (Jones, 2016; Jones & Abes, 2013; Jones & McEwen, 2003). The MMDI contains four elements, including the core, multiple social identities, identity salience, and contextual influences (see Jones & McEwen, 2000; Jones & Abes, 2013, for in-depth descriptions). Contextual influences include family background, sociocultural conditions, current experiences, and career decisions and life planning (Jones & Abes, 2013). Contextual influences are environments and social interactions that are also highlighted in the five dimensions of the culturally relevant leadership learning model (see Chapter 1) which include: (a) historical legacy of inclusion and exclusion, (b) compositional diversity, (c) psychological climate, (d) behavioral climate, and (e) organizational/structural aspects (Bertrand Jones et al., 2016).

As Jones (2016) stated, "the MMDI is intended as a developmental snapshot, rather than a fixed portrayal of identity, and suggests perceptions of one's identities and relative salience are constantly shifting in relation to changing contexts" (p. 26). Salience means the importance attached to a particular experience, idea, feeling, or identity (Jones & Abes, 2013). Salience also means the constant and frequent reminders you receive from those around you or from the messages in society. For example, the identities you think of right when you get out of bed are probably more salient to you. Some examples with salient gender or racial identities could include your clothing and what is perceived as being professional in society's standards.

In 2007, Abes, Jones, and McEwen reconceptualized MMDI. The reconceptualized model incorporates students' meaning-making filters to understand the depth and nuances of students' capacity of making meaning of contextual influences. You are able to understand your own capacities to understanding social identities in different contexts. As well as how those identities intersect with one another and make meaning from those inter-

Figure 2.1

Model of Multiple Dimensions of Identity (MMDI)

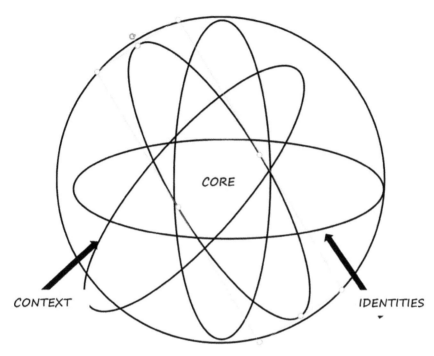

Adapted from Abes, Jones, & McEwen (2007); Jones & Abes (2013); Jones & McEwen (2000).

sections. Contextual influences include the relationship between students' meaning making of multiple identity dimensions and their external environments. Abes and colleagues (2007) noted context and environmental influences are connected to our own perceptions of identity. For example, we are not born with perceptions of ourselves as shy, interested in classical music, or charitable to others. Rather, such beliefs are determined by our observations of and interactions with others. The same is true for all of our social identities.

Dominant Versus Subordinated or Marginalized Identities

Dominant and subordinated are terms that describe social location of people based on their membership in a group or category of people who are either privileged or marginalized by societal systems of oppression (Davis & Harrison, 2014). People holding dominant identities often create the laws, structures, and social orders that people with marginalized identities have to abide by. Often, the larger society and institutions are controlled by these dominant groups and identities, and they decide how society should be organized. Dr. Beverly Daniel Tatum stressed that, "the dominant group has the greatest influence in determining the structure of society" (2017, p. 12). The power relationship between these two groups is vital to understanding privilege and how those who have privilege benefit. The dominant group basically holds all of the power in the relationship. Tatum points out that if the subordinate group does anything that does not align with the dominant group, then they are less than and often seen as inhumane. This power is also often invisible. Sometimes it's hard to point out the power imbalance because those in power often do not want to admit they have power because it benefits them. Therefore, some choose to not see it while those without power are forced to see whether they want to or not. As a result, this power imbalance in the relationship between those with dominant identities and those who hold subordinate identities becomes ingrained in our society and our understandings of social identities. When it becomes engrained, that means it becomes prevalent in many institutions and systems, like education, housing, and healthcare.

You can, and probably do, hold both dominant and subordinate identities. It might be difficult to understand exactly what dominant identities you may have but being Christian, male, and heterosexual are all dominant identities in Western society. Being Christian is dominant because many of societal norms are based on Christian values and expectations, for example, national holidays like Christmas are the norm for observing on our academic calendar, where Ramadan is not a national holiday and students have to make a request to their professors when observing this holiday. Being born as a minoritized race or ethnicity, identifying as a gender other than a *cisgender* man, a term for people whose gender identity matches their sex assigned at birth, or identifying as a sexuality other than heterosexual are seen as subordinate identities because they are marginalized identities.

Social Location

Social location is defined as the social position an individual holds within society and is based upon social characteristics deemed to be important by any given society (Sensoy & DiAngelo, 2017). Some of the social characteristics deemed to be important by U.S. society include social class and socioeconomic status, gender identity, sexual orientation, ethnicity, race, religion, and others. Researchers argue that the social location of an individual profoundly influences who they are and who they become, interactions with others, self-perception, opportunities, and outcomes (Davis & Harrison, 2014; Sensoy & DiAngelo, 2017).

For most people, nationality is an important part of their social location. For example, someone who likes to travel internationally may often be reminded of the degree to which their nationality influences their perceptions of the world, their likes and dislikes, and their tolerance for different behaviors and customs. This can also be true for U.S. citizens who travel to different regions of the country. In the next section, we will explore intersecting identities using a student, Karl, as an example.

KARL'S INTERSECTING IDENTITIES

We all hold multiple social positions in society and these positions do not cancel each other out; they interact in complex ways that must be explored and understood (Sensoy & DiAngelo, 2017). For example, when reflecting on how Karl (as you read below), makes meaning of his multiple identities, he must first acknowledge his personal identities and his understanding of those identities.

Karl as an Example

Karl is a senior at Southeast University majoring in sociology and criminal justice from Albany, Georgia. Karl identifies as cisgender man who is African American and gay. Karl was raised southern Baptist and his family is working class. Karl recognizes that issues can emerge for him as a leader who holds same/similar or very different identities from those who he engages with in the leadership process. Additionally, Karl must recognize his privileges and power dynamics as a student leader. Through reflection, he begins to consider how he will potentially navigate engaging in the leadership process and the role his identities play in how he makes meaning of his leadership experiences. His own worldviews may cause conflict with his understandings and experiences of leadership and the role of the leader and other expectations of him as a leader. Karl's reflection briefly outlines some of his own salient social identities and how these identities influence his leadership approaches and his ongoing reflection of his personal meaning making of the leadership process.

Karl's social identities as a Black gay cisgender man from Georgia can influence how he relates to others from similar or different identities. His understanding of his experiences and feelings as a gay Black man witnessing injustice can contribute to his own understandings of oppression in society. Karl might start to feel frustration towards those who cannot recognize their racial privilege or those who acknowledge it but also cannot recognize oppression or those who see the world through a colorblind lens. In a colorblind society, White people can effectively ignore racism in American life, justify the current social order, and feel more comfortable with their relatively privileged standing in society because they are unlikely to face disadvantages due to race (Fryberg & Stephens, 2010). Most racially minoritized people, however, who regularly encounter difficulties due to race, experience colorblind ideologies quite differently. Colorblindness creates a society that denies their negative racial experiences, rejects their cultural heritage, and invalidates their unique perspectives. These frustrations might also come into play when engaged in the leadership process with someone who he might perceive as having privileges based on their social identities.

Identity Reflection Activity

Using Table 2.1, consider how your own social identities impact your everyday life. There are is no right or wrong answer or even good or bad answer as you think about your social identities. Allow this reflection to help you better understand your own personal identity and your social identities. We often times don't just sit and reflect on how we define ourselves and what societal group memberships we hold. On the other hand, some of us think about this constantly and how being a member of a certain group or having a certain social identity impacts our daily lives. Society has created certain norms based on social identities and how we should behave, or how we are represented, or their value.

Next, we will revisit Karl as an example. When reflecting on his own worldview and how that might cause tensions, but also alignment with his own leadership approach, Karl first must understand his own worldview and how that knowledge has been constructed through his experiences. His salient identities (think MMDI) and experiences as a racially minoritized student on a predominately White campus, as Christian in a predominately Christian country, his gayness in a homophobic society, and his role as a cisgender man in a transphobic society have all shaped his worldview. His knowledge, or lack of knowledge, of oppression and privilege have been influenced by all of these identities and his development within these identities. Patton (2002) stressed that our understandings of our reality are socially constructed and culturally influenced. These understandings of

Table 2.1

Identifying Advantages and Disadvantages of Your Identities

Identity Category	How do you identify?	What benefits are you afforded?	What challenges have you experienced?	How often do you think about this identity?
Gender Identity				
Social Class				
Cultural background				
Race				
Ethnicity				
Religious Affiliation				
Educational Background				
Sexual orientation				
Age				
Ability Status				
Languages Spoken				
Physical Stature				
Nationality				
Immigration Status				

Adapted from Davis & Harris (2014).

society and the social construction can be dominant at any time and place (Patton, 2002). Therefore, this knowledge that Karl has constructed from these lived experiences shapes how he makes meaning of experiences and interactions during the leadership process (Bertrand Jones et al., 2016; Chunoo et al., 2019). Karl must also further acknowledge any biases he might have that could influence the leadership process. Recognizing these biases allows him to be conscious of his own social identities and their influences on him when he engages with others in the leadership process (Chunoo et al., 2019).

Karl, Power, and Privilege

As Karl continues to reflect on his own identities and how he might interact with different social identities and identities similar to his, he needs to consider how he would respond to those who hold different identities to him and how identities hold both privileges and power. Privilege and power must also be acknowledged in the leadership process in similar ways (Jones et al., 2013). Meaning, for those who hold different social identities than Karl, he must consider his role and positions of power and privileges based on his social identities (as a cisgender man, Christian, educated, etc.) and recognize his own actions of oppression, both intentionally and unintentionally. A consideration for Karl to be mindful of when thinking about his privileged identities are: how are others viewing him as a leader in relation to social identities and the power and privileges those identities hold?; what contextual influences, like behavioral (interaction across difference) or psychological (attitudes about difference) dimension of the campus environment, influence Karl's identity (see Chapter 1)? Karl also sees himself as a leader in the leadership process. In the next section we will explore the leadership identity development process.

What is your understanding of the leadership process and someone's role in the leadership process that might hold Karl's leadership position and social identities?

How do you make meaning of your own social identities and privileges in relation to the leadership process?

BARRIERS AND OPPORTUNITIES IN DEVELOPING A LEADERSHIP IDENTITY

There is currently a well-known model that situates leadership as an identity. The study that resulted in the leadership identity development (LID) model was conducted and is an opportunity to understand leadership development as an intersection of student development and leadership (Komives et al., 2005). The students identified to participate in the study were practicing a relational approach to leadership. Komives et al. (1998) defined relational leadership as "a process of people together attempting to accomplish change or make a difference to benefit the common good" (p. 21). Through the students' descriptions of their leadership journey and reflections on the ways they previously conceptualized leadership up to their current approach to leadership, the research team came to understand the students' leadership experiences—hence, the creation of the LID model. The findings from the study resulted in leadership identity as the primary focus for a six-stage development model (Komives et al., 2005). A leadership identity was found to develop in these six stages, with periods of transition between each. If we think back to Karl as he is developing his leadership identity he is impacted by group influences and how others perceive him as a leader. This impact of others views about him expanded Karl's view of leadership and how he identifies as a leader.

Table 2.2

Leadership Identity Development Model and Reflection Questions

LID Model Stage	Description of the Stage	Reflection Questions
Stage 1: **Awareness**	The first stage involves becoming aware that there are leaders "out there" who are external to self, such as a sport's coach, a parent, or a teacher.	When did you first become aware of leadership? Who was the first person you noticed to be a leader?
Stage 2: **Exploration/ Engagement**	This period of immersion in group experiences is usually to make friends; a time of learning to engage with others (e.g., girl scouts, boy scouts, church choir, dance team, club sports).	What group experiences did you have growing up that exposed you to concepts of leadership and leaders?

(Table continued on next page)

Table 2.2 (Continued)

Leadership Identity Development Model and Reflection Questions

LID Model Stage	Description of the Stage	Reflection Questions
Stage 3: Leader Identified	This stage views leadership as the actions of the positional leader of a group, an awareness of the hierarchical nature of relationships in groups.	Who was the first "good" leader in position of power and influence you noticed? What qualities did they exhibit that made them a "good" leader to you?
Stage 4: Leadership Differentiated	Leadership is beginning to be seen as non-positional and as a shared group process.	Have you engaged in a group process where you noticed leadership being practiced and it was not from someone in a formal leadership position?
Stage 5: Generativity	Generativity is a commitment to developing leadership in others and having a passion for issues or group objectives that the person wants to influence.	Have you noticed a mentor or influencer who has contributed to you developing your own leadership capacity or efficacy?
Stage 6: Integration/ Synthesis	Integration acknowledges the personal capacity for leadership in diverse contexts and claiming the identity as a leader without having to hold a positional role.	How do you imagine your leadership approach in different situations? What does your leadership approach look like even when you don't hold a title or position?

Adapted from Komives et al. (2005).

Barriers to Consider While Developing a Leadership Identity

It is necessary to understand how leadership learning influences an individual's engagement in the leadership process. We encourage you to reflect on past and present experiences that have shaped your understanding of leadership and leaders, how the experiences shaped you, and why these specific experiences have influenced you and not others. As this chapter has noted, leadership learning influences three internal aspects of a leader: identity, capacity, and efficacy. Identity is who a person believes they are and how society groups membership. More generally, identity constantly evolves and changes. A barrier to consider when developing a leadership identity is how it is socially constructed, complex, and multifaceted. Social identities all intersect with your leader identity. Leader identity is who a person believes they are as a leader (Guthrie et al., 2013). Leader identity motivates students to further engage in pursuing leader capacity and efficacy. In the next chapter, we will explore leadership and capacity.

PERSONAL REFLECTION

- What part of your identity do you think people first notice about you?
  - o What part of your identity are you most comfortable sharing with other people?
  - o What part of your identity are you least comfortable sharing with other people?
- What part of your identity are you most proud of?
  - o What part of your identity did you struggle the most with growing up?
- What part of other people's identities do you notice first?

DISCUSSION QUESTIONS

- Explain in your own words how identity relates to leadership and engaging in the leadership process.
- In what ways could increasing your understanding of your own intersecting identities influence how you understand others' identities?
- Consider your own identities and those that are more salient to you—how do those salient identities influence your leadership identity?

TAKING LEADERSHIP IDENTITY FURTHER

Activity #1: Social Identity Wheel

The Social Identity Wheel is popular activity that encourages you to identify and reflect on the various ways you identify socially, how those identities become visible or more keenly felt at different times, and how those identities impact the ways others perceive or treat you. Draw a wheel (or use a worksheet) to fill in various social identities (you can use Table 2.1 as a reference by naming how you identify in terms of your race, gender identity, sex, ability status, sexual orientation, etc.) and further categorize those identities based on which matter most in your self-perception and which matter most in others' perception of you. To add an additional layer to the activity, we encourage you to consider your LID and what stages of the model you have navigated through thus far. Reflect on what role social identities play in your leadership identity development process.

Activity #2: Identity Card and Reflection Activity

(Adapted from Osteen, Mills, & Wiborg, Florida State University, Center for Leadership & Social Change)

This activity is about you - the identities that make up who you are as a student, leader, and person in the world. Start with a deep breath and simply think about all the pieces that make you who you are.

1. Reflect on the following identities and descriptors …
   Identities easily seen and reacted to by others ….

   - Age
   - Ethnicity
   - Physical Capability
   - Emotional Capability
   - Physical Dimensions (height, weight, …)
   - Health
   - Introvert/Extrovert

- Language
- Sex
- Race
- Cognitive Capability
- Gender Expression
- Physical Appearance
- Social Role (Peacemaker, Rebel, etc.)
- Any other identities you would like to add ...

Identities known to us but not as readily visible ...

- Socioeconomic Class
- Past Trauma
- Relationship Status
- Religion/Spirituality
- Major
- Political Affiliation
- Significant Life Events
- Military Experience
- Education
- Work Experience
- Birth Order
- Geographical Origin
- Sexual Orientation
- Interests/Hobbies (art, music, sports, ...)
- Family Role (parent, daughter, aunt ...)
- Family Background
- Strengths
- Weaknesses
- Any other identities you would like to add...

2. Using 3 x 5 index cards, respond to the identities/descriptors that speak most to you and how you see yourself. For each descriptor/identity that speaks to you—write your specific response on a separate card. Try to create at least 15–20 cards.
3. Once you have written out your cards, sort them by these questions. Cards may have more than one marking, and yet, challenge yourself to think through the different impact each identity plays in how you understand yourself.

- Which of these characteristics and experiences are most central to how you define yourself? Identify no more than 1/3 of your cards.
    - o   Mark them with a Star *
- Which characteristics and experiences are you surprised by, most intrigued by?
    - o   Mark them with an Exclamation Point !
- Which of these characteristics and experiences brings you the most joy? Proud of?
    - o   Mark them with a Smiley Face ☺
- Which of these characteristics and experiences are most central to how others define you?
    - o   Mark them with an arrow -->

4. Based on your responses to these questions, create a visual image of you with your index cards. How would you display your cards in a manner that most reflects you?
5. Individual Reflection: Look at your pattern of cards and descriptors, how does this image describe you at this particular moment in time? How might this physical display of you looked differently a year ago? What about a year from now?
6. Share your reactions and responses to the following questions with others who have completed the activity:

- As you look at your words, markings, and patterns—what stands out to you?
- Which of your cards empowers your voice as a student?
- Which of your cards empowers your voice as a leader? As a community member?
- Which cards challenge or create conflict for you as a student or leader?

CHAPTER 3

CAPACITY

What Is My Leadership Ability?

Building off our reflection of identity, we must also explore and learn about what we believe we are capable of doing in the process of leadership, both as a leader and a follower. This chapter explores the knowledge, skills, and attitudes you have and how you can develop them in relation to how you engage in the process of leadership. As we move through this chapter consider the following questions:

- What do I believe is my overall leadership ability?
- What are the skills we need for society?
- How do you engage in the five exemplary practices we discuss?

LEADERSHIP AND LEADER CAPACITY DEFINED

This chapter explores a concept called capacity, which is connected to the activity of leadership and more specifically, the knowledge, skills, and attitudes you have developed in your leadership learning. As mentioned

Engaging in the Leadership Process:
Identity, Capacity, and Efficacy for College Students, pp. 33–45
Copyright © 2021 by Information Age Publishing
All rights of reproduction in any form reserved.

in this text, identity, capacity, and efficacy are intertwined with leadership and are important to who you are as a leader and how you engage with others in the leadership process. You may ask, why is capacity important to my leadership learning?

Believing in your overall ability to behave effectively in the leadership process is critical in being able to engage the way you want to. An incredible scholar and educator, Julie Owen (2012) discusses three beliefs of leadership educators that focus on leadership capacities. These include that the skills of leadership can and should be learned, leadership capacities are intertwined, and that learning environments can be intentionally created to help with the integration of knowledge, skills, and experiences.

Another way to think about it is your leadership capacity is the ability to retain knowledge, skills, and attitudes that enhance your ability to engage in the leadership process. Remember, capacity is not the same as potential. Leadership potential is realizing your ability to be a leader. Leadership capacity is already having the ability to be a leader, but developing the knowledge, skills, values, and attitude to be a leader. Something else to note is that leadership capacity models tend to focus more on individual skill development (leader development) rather than collaborative, relationship-oriented approaches (leadership development).

Knowing, Being, Doing

The three principles of knowing, being, and doing are used frequently in leadership development. Referring to the relational foundation of the leadership process (Komives et al., 2013), you must know yourself and how others in the leadership process may view things differently. Being ethical, inclusive, caring, and authentic is important, which relates to the being part of leadership. How do you make decisions that reflect your being? Acting in socially responsible ways is part of doing that is critical, actually carrying out actions to fulfill the doing aspect of leadership. The concept of knowing, being, and doing is also framed that leadership development starts with knowing about leadership, proceeds to being a leader, and culminates with doing leadership by interacting with followers to create positive, sustainable change. One way to enhance your leadership capacity is by learning how scholars have framed leadership over the years. This will develop your leadership knowledge, enhance your leadership skills, and allow you to reflect on your values and attitudes regarding how you engage in leadership, and how you act as a leader. Digging into the five practices of exemplary leadership and leadership competencies not only enhances your leadership knowledge but will also jump-start your leadership skill-building.

Five Practices of Exemplary Leadership

After decades of research, in 1987 two scholars, Jim Kouzes and Barry Posner, proposed five practices of exemplary leadership. These five exemplary practices are what successful leaders have exhibited when they were at their "personal best" (Kouzes & Posner, 2012, p. 23). With data from interviews with thousands of leaders, these practices emerged. The focus of the interviews was for the leader to reflect on a time when they were at their personal best as a leader. Before we dig into the practices Kouzes and Posner found, let's pause for consideration.

> Reflect on a time you were engaged in a project where you felt you were at your personal best. What were you working on? Who were you working with? What were the skills you were exhibiting during this time? Were you acting as a leader? A follower?

The five practices of exemplary leadership that emerged from thousands of interviews are: (1) Model the way; (2) Inspire a shared vision; (3) Challenge the process; (4) Enable others to act; and (5) Encourage the heart (Kouzes & Posner, 2012, 2017, 2018). Table 3.1 provides brief descriptions of each of these five practices.

Table 3.1

Five Practices of Exemplary Leadership

Practice	Brief Description
Model the Way	Actions speak louder than words
	Demonstrate commitment
Inspire a Shared Vision	Have vision of change
	Ability to share vision
Challenge the Process	Uses change and innovation
Enable Others to Act	Acknowledges that accomplishments are not the result of a single person
	Develops others
Encourage the Heart	Recognition and celebration
	Fosters strong sense of community

Adapted from Kouzes, J. & Posner, B. (2012). *The Leadership Challenge* (5th ed.). Jossey-Bass.

The five practices are a good way to explore leadership skills broadly. These may read as ways of being an efficient leader. We would encourage you to consider how these also are influential practices in the leadership process, no matter what role you are in. Each practice can be enhanced by digging deep and committing to actions to enhance your skills in these areas. Below are specific ways in which each practice can be enhanced (Kouzes & Posner, 2012).

Practice #1: Model the Way

- Think about the words you speak and then act congruently
- Remember that collaboration and trust is nurtured and not forced. Leaders enact, not just simply act
- Refine values by finding your voice and supporting shared ideals
- Set an example by aligning behaviors with shared values

Practice #2: Inspire a Shared Vision

- Passionately believe you, as a leader, can make a difference
- Remember that leadership is a dialogue, not a monologue
- Imagine the future by visualizing exciting and stimulating possibilities
- Recruit others in a common vision by appealing to shared expectations

Practice #3: Challenge the Process

- Search for opportunities to change the status quo
- Remember that innovative thinking is critical to change
- Search for opportunities by taking initiative and looking for groundbreaking ways to improve
- Test and take risks by constantly generating small wins and learning from your experience

Practice #4: Enable Others to Act

- Actively involve others and build collaborative teams
- Remember that the people who make a difference in our lives are the ones who care and demonstrate this at every opportunity

- Foster collaboration by creating trust and facilitating relationships
- Strengthen others by developing their competence and skills

Practice #5: Encourage the Heart

- As a leader, make people feel like an important part of the process
- Remember the Golden Rule, treat people as you wish to be treated
- Acknowledge contributions by showing appreciation for individual excellence and collective achievements of the group
- Celebrate successes and achievements by creating a sense of community

Now that you have learned about the five exemplary leadership practices, did any of them emerge during the time you felt you were your personal best as a leader? Is there a practice that you feel you are naturally good at?

Each of the five exemplary practices is comprised of a multitude of individual competencies. Thinking more specifically about leadership competencies and which ones should be a part of your leadership development is part of the journey (and fun).

Competencies as Skills

Competencies are defined as "the collection of knowledge, skills and attitudes" (Mulder et al., 2008, p. 8) that contribute to one's ability to complete a task and overall behavior. If you remember how capacity was defined, there are clear similarities. The language of competencies is utilized across various organizations and is especially prevalent in educational settings, businesses, and professional associations (Conger & Ready, 2004). In the early stages of leadership development, skills approach (Katz, 1955; Mumford et al., 2000) was the focus of how to best develop leaders. The skills approach to leadership development believes that specific skills can be enhanced to increase a leader's ability to be effective. Yes, the development of skills is important, but it is not the only way to develop your leadership capacity. Competencies are skills that develop ability, but also have dimensions of behavior, knowledge, and value. For example, competencies focused on personal behavior include confidence, initiative, resilience, and follow-through. Thinking of competencies holistically in regards to development will enhance your leadership learning.

Leadership Competencies

Based on more than five years of extensive research, *The Student Leadership Competencies Guidebook* includes 60 leadership competencies for the 21st century (Seemiller, 2013). This list of competencies emerged through analyzing nearly 18,000 learning outcomes (what the goal of learning in the programs are) in manuals of 522 academic programs in U.S. colleges and universities, focusing on all industries, and jobs. Seemiller and Murray (2013) stated they had two objectives in this research. One was to simply develop a comprehensive list of leadership competencies across multiple disciplines. The second was to understand which competencies students need to engage in to better prepare them for leadership positions in their future careers. The result of this massive project was 60 leadership competencies. These competencies are categorized into eight clusters: learning and reasoning, self-awareness and development, interpersonal interaction, group dynamics, civic responsibility, communication, strategic planning, and personal behavior (Seemiller, 2013). Further, each competency includes four dimensions that reflect levels of learning and the holistic nature of competencies in practice. These include the knowledge (content), value (belief), ability (skill or motivation), and behavior (action). Figure 3.1 shows the clusters of leadership competencies with the dimensions of learning.

Examining the four broad dimensions, clusters of the competencies, and how they represent your leadership capacity is a good way to build on the five exemplary practices discussed early. Whether it is in a specific class or student organization, your leadership learning is essentially your development of leadership capacity due to the specific experience you have. It could be a specific dimension or multiple dimensions depending on the specific situation. For example, imagine you oversee the development and execution of a new member program for a student organization you have been involved with for two years. Although you are serving in a leader role, how will you develop during this experience? Will you focus on your ability? Sharpen your behavior in planning? Increase your knowledge? Or focus on the process of the new member program evolve somehow? Deliberately reflecting on the dimensions of skill development while engaging in a leadership experience will increase your leadership capacity greatly.

Figure 3.1

Student Leadership Competencies Clusters

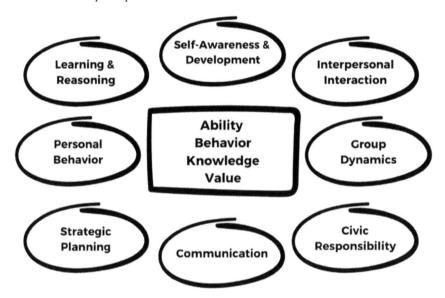

Adapted representation of the student leadership competency model from Seemiller and Murray (2013).

Now that you have learned about the five exemplary leadership practices, did any of them emerge during the time you felt you were your personal best as a leader? Is there a practice that you feel you are naturally good at?

Within these 8 clusters of competencies, there are a total of 60 leadership competencies (Seemiller & Murray, 2013). These 60 leadership competencies specify ways to sharpen your leadership skills. As you take a look at the list in Table 3.2, put a check by the competencies you feel you are already strong in and star the ones you would like to further develop.

Enhancing your leadership capacity by developing competencies will help you continue in your leadership learning journey. Now that you know more specifics about the exemplary practices and competencies, let's go a bit further into the potential challenges and opportunities in developing your leadership capacity.

Table 3.2

Leadership Competencies

Learning and Reasoning	Others' Contributions	Strategic Planning
Research	Productive Relationships	Goals
Analysis	Providing Feedback	Mission
Decision Making	Supervision	Organization
Evaluation		Plan
Idea Generation	**Group Dynamics**	Vision
Other Perspectives	Creating Change	
Problem Solving	Group Developments	**Personal Behavior**
Reflection and Application	Organizational Behavior	Confidence
Systems Thinking	Power Dynamics	Ethics
Synthesis		Excellence
		Follow-Through
Self-Awareness & Development	**Civic Responsibility**	Functioning Independently
Personal Contributions	Diversity	Initiative
Personal Values	Inclusion	Positive Attitude
Receiving Feedback	Others' Circumstances	Resilience
Self-Development	Service	Responsibility for Personal Behavior
Self-Understanding	Social Justice	Responding to Ambiguity
Scope of Competence	Social Responsibility	Responding to Change
Interpersonal Interaction	**Communication**	
Appropriate Interaction	Advocating for a Point of View	
Collaboration	Conflict Negotiation	
Empathy	Facilitation	
Empowerment	Listening	
Helping Others	Nonverbal Communication	
Mentoring	Writing	
Motivation	Verbal Communication	

BARRIERS AND OPPORTUNITIES IN DEVELOPING LEADERSHIP CAPACITY

Barrier of Using a Deficit Frame

Dominant narratives about minoritized identities are often framed from a deficit perspective, perpetuating the harmful notion that those with minoritized identities are lacking in some important aspect and therefore are not fit for leadership. Deficit perspectives often reinforce binary conceptualizations of leadership (e.g., leader vs. follower). Building leadership capacity by positioning your cultural backgrounds and life experiences as assets in leadership is critical. Yosso's (2005) community cultural wealth model expands the concept of wealth beyond the financial to include six other forms of capital including aspirational, familial, linguistic, navigational, resistant, and social capital.

Aspirational capital are the hopes and dreams you have; how do these hopes and dreams motivate you? Familial capital are the personal networks you may have, perhaps from extended family and friends; how do your family and friends support you? Linguistic capital are the communication and language skills you have; how does speaking another language benefit an organization you are a part of? Navigational capital are skills to make meaning of complex (educational) spaces; when have you had to navigate complex situations in the past and what did you learn from that experience? Resistant capital are experiences communities of color have in securing collective freedom and equality; what skills have you obtained by working for equality? Social capital, the sixth in Yosso's (2005) community cultural wealth model, are peers and social contacts; how can you call on your friends and colleagues to support, encourage, and assist?

Including these additional forms of capital can broaden the strengths diverse individuals bring to the leadership process. Strengthening your intersectional identities (e.g., race, ethnicity, religion) by building awareness and expanding your perspective of the assets and resources you have and can apply to leadership processes and positively influence your development.

Barrier of Focusing on the Individual

Leadership competency models tend to focus on individual skill development (leader development) and less on collaboration and relationship-oriented approaches (leadership development). Bolden and Gosling (2006) state, "competency frameworks tend to reinforce individualistic practices that dissociate leaders from the relational environment in which they operate and could, arguably, inhibit the emergence of more inclusive and collective forms of leadership" (p. 13). For example, if a training for a student organization only focuses on individual skill development, but nothing tending to relational processes, the student organization members may have difficulties applying individual skills to collective processes, like planning a community service event with many partners. It is important to remain mindful of environment, context, and relationships within leadership situations. This is highlighted in the five dimensions of the culturally relevant leadership learning model (see Chapter 1). For example, what contextual influences, like the historical legacy of exclusion/inclusion of the organization (see Chapter 1), influence your leadership competency? Also, it is vital to learn how to leverage our own competencies along with the competencies of others for effective group functioning.

Opportunity for Collective Capacity

Although a barrier of leadership capacity is the focus on individual development, there is also great opportunity in exploring collective capacity. More specifically the ways individuals can contribute to how groups and communities develop collective competencies. The social change model of leadership development, for example, offers three levels of development: individual, group, and community (Astin & Astin, 1996), in which competency development at the group and community levels may be useful both for the process and outcome of leadership. Collective competencies are an essential part of our global society and should be focused on as part of individual competency development.

Opportunity for Development of Leadership Capacity

An opportunity to really sharpen your leadership capacity is developing your emotional intelligence (Goleman, 1998; Mayer & Salovey, 1993). Emotional intelligence focuses on your self-awareness and understanding how your emotional skills affects your thinking and action. Emotionally intelligent leadership (Shankman et al., 2015) builds off the concept of emotional intelligence and focuses on college students (that is you!). There are three facets of emotionally intelligent leadership including consciousness of self, consciousness of others, and consciousness of context. Within these three facets there are 19 specific capacities in which you can develop in relation to your emotions (Shankman et al., 2015). Emotional Intelligence and emotionally intelligent leadership are essential in developing leadership capacity as it is in relation to others. Although you do not need to master all capacities, it is important to understand how awareness and regulation of emotions in different situations are critical to the leadership process. Being able to read a room (and situation) is a skill vital for challenging leadership situations.

In reflecting on barriers and opportunities in developing leadership capacity, what skills do we individually need for society? How can we be best equipped as leaders? How will your lived experiences and leadership capacity make the world a better place?

Developing your leadership ability is important to your leadership learning journey. Being intentional about what knowledge, skills, and attitudes you want to have in order to be an ethical leader who can be trusted is critical.

PERSONAL REFLECTION

- What do you think are the most important leadership capacities (knowledge, skills, and experiences) you possess currently?
- What leadership capacities (knowledge, skills, and experiences) do you need to work on developing?
- What is the biggest personal barrier you face in developing leadership capacity?

DISCUSSION QUESTIONS

- How does identity influence (either helps or hinders) our ability to develop our leadership capacities?
- What experiences (individually or in a group) have you had in developing leadership capacities? In what way has that connected to your leadership identity?
- Does leadership capacity influence your personal definition of leadership? If so, how?

TAKING LEADERSHIP CAPACITY FURTHER

Activity #1: Leadership Competencies Self-Development Plan

Student leadership competencies are one way to focus on developing and identifying your overall leadership ability. Creating a self-development plan focused on competencies will help guide your leadership learning and increase your leadership capacity. First, identify five competencies you would like to intentionally develop. When choosing these competencies, think about those that would be valuable to you personally, in a potential organization you are a part of, and in a future career. Use the table below to write out your self-development plan for your leadership learning. First, list what competencies you will focus on, what cluster they fit into and in what context this will be (personally, in an organization, in the community, for your future career). Next, write out specific plans in how you will develop them in the short-term (think approximately 6 months) and longer-term (1–2 years). Be specific in how you will proceed with a plan to strengthen your chosen competencies.

Competency	Context	Short-Term (6 Months)	Longer-Term (1-2 years)
ex: Nonverbal Communication	Organization	I will reflect on the nonverbal communication I saw occurring at organizational meetings by recording them in a journal	In the next year, when I serve as a leader, I will ask a peer and my advisor to give me constructive feedback on my nonverbal communication

Activity #2: How Do You Spend Your Time?

Related to believing in your ability as a leader is how you model the way, which is one of Five Exemplary Practices (Kouzes & Posner, 2018). How you spend your time is critical to modeling the way and developing your ability as a leader. This activity will help you explore the alignment of the values you claim to have and the way you spend your time. First, think about your top personal values (HINT: If you are stuck, you can find lists of personal values by simply searching on the internet). Write 3–4 of these top personal values down on a piece of paper. Next, open your calendar (whether that is in a digital or paper format). Look at what you have scheduled and jot down what you do during your unscheduled time (being on social media, having meals with friends, streaming shows, going out socializing, etc.). Review your calendars and think about how well your actions and time spent align with the values you say you hold. Identify one way you spend your time that aligns well with your stated values and one that is not in alignment. How does being intentional with how you spend your time model the way for others? How does aligning the time you spend with your values increase your leadership capacity?

CHAPTER 4

EFFICACY

What Can I Do?

This chapter explores a concept called efficacy, which is connected to the process of leadership and more specifically, your belief in your ability to engage in the leadership process or through a leadership position. As we move through this chapter consider the following questions:

- What identities, skills, abilities, knowledge, and values do you have that contributes to the leadership process?
- What positive leadership experiences with efficacy development have you had? Negative leadership experiences?
- How does societal or external messaging influence your beliefs about your leadership abilities?
- What are strategies for maintaining or increasing your leadership self-efficacy?

Engaging in the Leadership Process:
Identity, Capacity, and Efficacy for College Students, pp. 47–64
Copyright © 2021 by Information Age Publishing

Consider a time when you were engaging in some sort of activity that was new for you. Maybe it was your first time you rode a bike, played a new sport or instrument, started a job, or something similar. Was your belief in your ability to be successful with that activity 100% from the beginning? Most likely not, you practiced, needed time to learn, had a family member, friend, coach, supervisor, or mentor teach you, and then your belief in your ability to successfully do it increased. However, your identities and environment may have influenced this belief. For example, maybe you came from a family with a long history of being successful at basketball. From a young age, you were affirmed that you would be a basketball player and you might have been more likely to join pick-up games around your neighborhood or at school. Your identity—I am a basketball player—and your capacity—I have the skills, knowledge, and practice to play basketball—were enhanced, which linked to a possible belief in your ability to perform well as a basketball player.

This chapter explores a concept called efficacy, which is connected to leadership and more specifically, your belief in your ability to engage in the leadership process or through a leadership position. As we have mentioned throughout this text, identity, capacity, and efficacy are intertwined with leadership; these concepts matter to who you are as a leader and how you engage with others in the leadership process. Why is efficacy important to college student leadership learning? Research conducted by Denzine (1999) found student leaders' efficacy beliefs:

- Affect choices in involvement,
- Impact what and how much student leaders learn,
- Determine performance and achievement levels,
- Influence psychological well-being, and
- Contribute to collective efficacy perceptions (i.e., beliefs about the group's potential for success).

In addition, college is a time in life where transitions and life choices often manifest. Life can bring unexpected challenges and your path may have more adversity or taxing situations than you expected. Your efficacy beliefs may influence the actions, decisions, responses to obstacles or environmental conditions, and resilience (Bandura, 1997). Further, in group or organizational settings, your efficacy beliefs influence the empowerment and mobilization of others to create change, both in their individual lives and in the community or society. More broadly, leadership efficacy moves students toward creating change (Osteen et al., 2016). People tend to avoid tasks they believe they won't accomplish or are not good at, and so belief in your abilities (or the group's abilities) to successfully engage in the leadership process, in order to create change, is crucial to consider (Denzine, 1999; Wagner, 2011).

Your internal belief in your ability to do something, like leading, can reflect goals, choices, aspirations, effort, persistence, and endurance through difficulties (McCormick et al., 2002). As a person grows in their capacity (increases their skills to lead in a specific situation, as discussed in Chapter 3) and receives validation of their efforts, self-efficacy grows. A person's self-efficacy meter is increased as you keep practicing and learning from both successes and failures (Crosby, 2017). However, a person's efficacy beliefs are not necessarily an accurate portrayal of their capabilities to do something (Goddard et al., 2004). We must have a healthy balance in our beliefs by understanding that leadership is a life-long process of engaging with others and differs from context to context. By understanding the difference between leadership capacity and leadership efficacy, we can have a deeper understanding of what we need to individually or collectively work on to be a better leader, group, organization, collaborative, or team. You can have capacity, but if you don't believe you will be successful, you might not act. In comparison, you can have a belief in your ability, but if you don't have the skills, you might not be prepared to act.

LEADERSHIP AND LEADER EFFICACY DEFINED

Efficacy, specifically in relation to leadership, is derived primarily from the social cognitive theory of motivation and behavior by Bandura. Bandura (1997) is the most cited theorist on efficacy and defines it as a belief in one's ability to successfully accomplish a specific task in a particular context. Bandura called other theorists to explore the concept of efficacy in the context of other domains. Efficacy has been linked to leadership because of the need to engage in a wide range of tasks during challenging situations that occur while engaging in the leadership process. You may be able to see how personal beliefs in your skills, abilities, and knowledge would be a predictor of how you would perform in a given situation. Likewise, if you have greater confidence or inner belief in your ability, you may be more open to applying or being interested in either positional or non-positional roles or experiences. As a result, Hannah and colleagues (2008) composed a framework for leadership and leader efficacy. Leadership efficacy is a belief in your ability to be successful in collective groups and engage in the leadership process across positional boundaries. Leadership efficacy calls for an awareness of the people you are working with and the context you are working in.

Hannah and colleagues (2008) proposed that, to have an enhanced leadership efficacy, we must understand leader efficacy, which requires an identification of the difference between the two. Leader efficacy can be defined as the "Leaders' (followers') beliefs in their perceived capabilities to organize the positive psychological capabilities, motivation, means, collective resources, and courses of action required to attain effective, sustainable performance across their various leadership roles, demands, and contexts" (Hannah et al., 2008, p. 670). This definition does not mention leader's confidence in working with others or engaging in a group with followers. Leadership efficacy can be viewed as a more team or collective approach to enhancing the belief in one's ability to participate in the leadership process rather than an individual leader (Hannah et al., 2008). It is more complex and multi-layered and includes leader efficacy, follower efficacy, and collective efficacy in the hope to transition into collective positive performance (Hannah et al., 2008).

In other words, "leader efficacy is tied to internal beliefs about serving in a formal or positional role, whereas leadership efficacy addresses beliefs associated with group processes that extend beyond specific roles" (Dugan, 2017, p. 16). This distinction is important and goes back to why language is crucial to understanding leadership. If we confuse the two, we may undervalue or overvalue our views on if we can successfully contribute to a group, organization, and community. Leadership is more about the collective processes we engage in as people to work towards a common goal or change. For example, conflict is something that tends to come up when working with a group over a period of time and relates to the leadership process. Conflict can be a barrier or opportunity to whatever goal or change your group is working towards. If you are someone with a high belief in your ability to manage conflict, link conflict management to the leadership process, and successfully get the group to engage in/through the conflict, you will have a higher leadership efficacy.

If you are someone who has a low belief in your ability to manage conflict and also acknowledge conflict is important to leadership, you may seek leadership workshops or readings on how to increase your ability to manage conflict. Once you seek out those resources and practice, your leadership efficacy should increase. However, this is different than leader efficacy because conflict management is not always tied to a formal or positional role, but can be if the role often has to be the one called on to respond to conflict situations (i.e., human resource staff members, resident assistants, fraternity or sorority conduct boards, etc.). You can actually be in a positional role that requires skills in conflict management and not enact behaviors that could be helpful to your group's process, resulting in an undesirable outcome. Sometimes we oversimplify an issue or concern about leading—there is self-doubt in applying for a student leader position because of various reasons—so you might say that person has a low leader efficacy. However, once you ask deeper questions, you may see there are real doubts about their leadership skills or capacity to be effective with a group of peers. In this text, we will focus on leadership efficacy because we know everyone reading this book is associated with group processes that extend beyond specific roles. Skills and capacity can be grown or developed, and often develop through challenging experiences that stretch our knowledge, capacity, or identity as a leader.

Self-Efficacy

So, is self-efficacy the same as self-confidence? No, and here is why. It is important to understand the difference between self-efficacy and self-confidence when thinking about applying this to your leadership experiences (Dugan, 2017; McCormick et al., 2002). Self-confidence is a general sense of competence and is often considered a fixed trait, whereas self-efficacy is a personal belief in your ability to be successful with a specific task or process. This means it is specific to a context, not general, and changes over time depending on your growth and development. For example, you may have a high internal belief in your ability to drive a car, but if you change that task to driving a semi-truck, your self-efficacy might (and should) be low until you build your skills and capacities in driving a semi-truck. Another difference between these constructs is that self-confidence is often associated with an external portrayal of your sense of competence, whereas self-efficacy is an internal belief that might lead to portrayal but doesn't necessarily have to. Here's an example to show you why this distinction is so important:

> Ruby (she/her/hers) signed up for a leadership course because it met a requirement she needed to graduate. She also is a junior and was hoping to apply to be the service chair for her business organization. She believes that service is crucial to any business because of the need to understand, support, and partner with the local community. She has not had a formal leadership role in the organization before but consistently signs up for service opportunities and enjoys getting to connect with community members. Ruby does believe that she has the ability to lead in this role, but is often characterized as quiet and hasn't had time to vocalize her interest. She also questions if this is needed since she will just go through the application process that is set-up to apply for the role. However, she recently found out that the current service chair has already spoken to other people in the organization who they think would be good for the role and she was not one of them. She now questions her value to the organization and if others think she will be good in the role.

It can be easy in this example to project some sort of blame, either on Ruby for not vocalizing her interest and questioning her value to the organization or the current service chair for not recognizing Ruby's commitment to service and her ability to be great in the role. Since this example is void of context, we won't attempt to analyze it too deeply, outside of understanding that your internal belief and voice are connected, even if your internal voice is never externalized to others or spoken. It is so important because you or someone you know may have a willingness to engage in a leadership role, and either you or they don't vocalize it because there may be doubt present.

Social Identity Considerations

Leadership is a social process and not void of issues of power, privilege, marginalization, stereotyping, and microaggressions. The Multi-Institutional Study of Leadership (MSL) launched in 2006 to comprehensively assess the effectiveness of leadership programs on leadership and college student outcomes (Dugan et al., 2013). This study of over 60,000 students and programs from over 52 colleges and universities explored leadership development, as well as shared evidence-based leadership learning and practices. MSL found that leadership efficacy was a key predictor of gains in leadership capacity, as well as if students actually utilized leadership behaviors in their contexts and environments. MSL confirmed that leadership efficacy contributes to "increase motivation to enact leadership behaviors, gains in leadership capacity as well as performance, and the ability to reject negative external feedback including stereotype threat" (Dugan et al., 2013, p. 16). Further, the findings exhibited across all demographic groups leadership self-efficacy was cultivated through positional leadership roles and socio-cultural conversations (Dugan et al., 2013).

The MSL data was used in other ways to determine efficacy for specific identity groups as well, including commuter students, Students of Color, and women in science, technology, engineering, and math fields (Dugan et al., 2008; Dugan et al., 2013; Kodama & Dugan, 2013). In the past, research studies have shown that leadership self-efficacy is low for Students of Color and women (Dugan & Komives, 2010; Kodama & Dugan, 2013). Turman and colleagues (2018), stated,

> People's social identities and lived experiences influence their beliefs in their abilities to practice leadership. In addition, power constructs and contextual influences (e.g., compositional diversity of a group, locality) that shape one's social position have implications for the development of leadership self-efficacy. (p. 66)

Based on this quote, we could ask the following questions about Ruby's interest in getting more involved in the business organization: What contextual influences, like compositional diversity of the organization (see

Chapter 1), influence Ruby's leadership self-efficacy? Considering the sociohistorical influences of business as a field, could Ruby being a woman influence this scenario? What areas of campus has Ruby found meaningful involvement? Is this organization an involvement that connects most to her major and future or current career goals? If yes, how do her beliefs in her ability to lead relate to her future career aspirations? These questions highlight the complexity of leadership self-efficacy because of how internal beliefs and feelings are not void from the realities of our social systems.

However, efficacy is considered to be a primary mechanism of human agency (Bandura, 1997; Hannah et al., 2008); meaning by understanding the details and sources of our beliefs, we can act, adapt, or change. Moreover, efficacy beliefs can be explained like a negative/downward spiral or a positive/upward spiral, where your leadership self-efficacy beliefs can intensify either direction (Machida & Schaubroeck, 2011). The positive or upward spiral can encourage an internal voice to pursue difficult or complex tasks, where the negative or downward spiral can encourage self-doubt. Later in this chapter, we will highlight strategies for encouraging positive spirals and responding to negative self-efficacy beliefs, through exploring opportunities and barriers developing leadership self-efficacy. Leader efficacy is something that can be developed and increased through specific identifiable strategies (Hannah et al., 2008).

Collective Efficacy

People change their lives for the better not only through self-development but by *acting together* to alter adverse institutional practices. If the practices of social systems impede or undermine the personal development of some sectors of society, then a large part of *the solution lies in changing the adverse practices of social systems through the exercise of collective efficacy.* To shape their social future, people must believe themselves capable of accomplishing significant *social change,* which rarely comes easily. (emphasis added; Bandura, 1997, p. 33)

Collective efficacy, as a concept and process, provides critical hope in responding to inequitable systems and institutional practices. The emphasis on collective efficacy moves conceptualizations of leadership from an individual to a collective or unified perspective. Collective efficacy is defined as a "group's shared belief in its conjoint capabilities to organize and execute the courses of action required to produce specific levels of accomplishments" (Hannah et al., 2008, p. 680). The group can be an organization, club, team, coalition, committee, community, office, institution, or even a nation of people; the factors linking to collective efficacy include a combination of knowledge and competencies in the group, the group structuring or coordination of activities, strategies utilized, and the interactions of the group members working towards a common purpose (Bandura, 1997). Bandura (1997) stated the following, which can still be applied to the current times we live in: "The new dimensions of change, which have far-reaching consequences, call for strong commitment to shared purposes and wide-ranging solutions to social problems ... achieved only through the unified effort of people who have the skills, the sense of collective efficacy, and the incentives to shape their future" (p. 520). Working towards social change coalesces group members' interests and skills to support shared values and collective goals (Bandura, 1997).

How sure am I that my community, group, or organization will be successful in creating change, rooted in our purpose as a group? *This does not necessarily have to be the original goal or change that was intended.*

Bandura (1997) delineates that collective efficacy can be translated from generation to generation. We benefit from those who came before us and collectively fought against social inequities, and those who come after us will be shaped by our collective work; therefore, it is crucial to develop our collective efficacy. Movements like women's suffrage, labor rights, civil rights, the Stonewall riots, Chicano civil rights, March for Our Lives, and Black Lives Matter could not result in the impact they had or continue to have without a collective belief in their ability to create change, even amongst the on-going set-backs. College students have a long-standing tradition of involvement in movements advancing social justice and holding their institutions accountable. For example, at Fisk University, a Historically Black College and University (HBCU), starting in the 1920s, Black students demanded faculty, staff, and administrators to center their identities and lived experiences into the curriculum; they advocated for their social, cultural practices to be linked to literacy in higher education (Kynard, 2013). These students engaged in writing policy, initiated discussions with faculty and administrative committees, and persuaded large groups and key partners to ensure HBCUs were about the advancement of Black communities, rather than an institution designed by "white architects" (Kynard, 2013, p. 40). Fisk University student protestors created a movement, along with other students across the United States, for HBCUs to be sites of resistance for social change, pushing against hierarchal structures and systems of oppression. Marginalized communities have been leading through collectivist ways from the start, including students at institutions of higher education; your beliefs in your capabilities can be enhanced by understanding the local and global history of working towards social change, as well as the current ideas and practices from other organizations or movements (Owen et al., 2017).

BARRIERS AND OPPORTUNITIES IN
DEVELOPING LEADERSHIP EFFICACY

Since college student leadership self-efficacy can either "expand or limit the choices...when considering whether to take on a challenging group task or new leadership experience (e.g., those with low self-efficacy for leadership are less likely to engage in such experiences)" (Wagner, 2011, p. 92), then we have to understand how to develop our leadership self-efficacy. Although there is a large number of leadership books, trainings, programs, and courses for college students focused on building capacity, like skill development or learning leadership theories, those do not automatically translate to developing your leadership self-efficacy or collective efficacy in a group. It often requires engaging in real leadership experiences, coupled with intentional reflection or processing of your experiences (Wagner, 2011). As seen in Table 4.1, Bandura (1997) shared four sources that shape efficacy beliefs: (1) direct or mastery experience, (2) vicarious experience, (3) verbal persuasion and affirmation, and 4) assessment of physiological and affective states.

Table 4.1

Leadership Self-Efficacy Sources

Efficacy Sources (Derived from Bandura, 1997)	*Leadership Applications*	*Simplified Definition*
Direct or Mastery Experiences	Experiences that promote collaboration, leadership learning, and skill development	Your/Our Leadership Experiences
Vicarious Experience	Observation of others engaging in the leadership process, with or without a formal title/role	Witnessing Other Leadership Experiences
Verbal Persuasion and Affirmation	Receiving encouragement, affirmation, and feedback from others' (mentors, friends, teammates, teachers, advisors, etc.)	Affirmation and Feedback on Leadership Experiences
Assessment of Physiological and Affective States	Understanding your/our moods, feelings, energy, and stress levels in relation to engaging in the leadership process	Internal Thoughts and Feelings on Leadership Experiences

Your/Our Leadership Experiences

Involvement and engagement in meaningful experiences provide opportunities to learn new skills, recognize your abilities or the groups' abilities, and practice collaborative leadership. Leadership engagement can be defined as learning by doing, as described in Chapter 1 (Guthrie & Jenkins, 2018), and is included as an efficacy source. However, we hope you do not read this efficacy source as a need to overextend yourself and apply for every leadership position, training, or opportunity. The experiences should be purposeful and connected to your passions, addressing issues that affect your community, or may be connected to your career or major. At the same time, we have to understand there are access considerations to take into account when thinking about leadership experiences. Being a college student and having access to structured leadership learning opportunities is a privilege, rooted in a commitment that most universities believe in graduating prepared leaders that address community needs.

Barriers. Leadership learning is emphasized on college campuses. However, access to those opportunities is not always equitable. For example, some students have to work full-time jobs or are a parent, where involvement opportunities may not be scheduled at an accessible time, creating a barrier for leadership engagement. Furthermore, leadership programs or organizations can require payment to access workshops, retreats, or experiences. Traditional leadership opportunities require an application and selection process. Process-wise, this means you first have to learn about it through marketing or recruitment, have the time and persistence to complete the application materials, and then get selected, in which others have the power to say who is included or not included. This can be limiting but by broadening our conceptualization of what leadership is, we have meaningful experiences that relate to our ability to engage in the leadership process.

Opportunities. Leadership is not just focused on positional leaders, and there are many opportunities to enact change beyond the formalization of leadership roles or organizations. We are not saying to ignore the real power authority has on creating change, but we are saying there are ways to learn about the flow of power and how to collaborate with others to create meaningful change. For example, advocacy, activism, and service should be included in our conceptualization of what leadership experiences are; they should be celebrated. College students come to college having been activists, holding politicians accountable, impacting individual lives through service—but it should not be about individual skills, but collective capacity to learn, do, create, and connect through these experiences. A strategy for increasing your leadership self-efficacy is to couple your experiences with intentional reflection and meaning making based on socialization, identities, comparative considerations, collaboration, and relationality. Even if the outcome of your group failed to reach a goal, your group can have a heightened belief in their abilities by processing the experience.

Witnessing Other Leadership Experiences

Research on leadership self-efficacy also states that if you observe others engaging in the leadership process, your leadership self-efficacy can increase. This is not surprising considering leadership observation, as discussed in Chapter 1, is included in the leadership learning framework (Guthrie & Jenkins, 2018). We can learn by observing leadership processes we are not directly involved in.

Barriers. Leadership research fails to describe the value of witnessing a leader or team fail at what they are seeking, then identifying how they move forward, exhibiting positive ways to navigate challenges. For example, Stacey Abrams in 2018 was the democratic nominee for the Georgia gubernatorial election but lost without conceding the election. Abrams went on to deliver the response to the State of the Union address in 2019 and founded Fair Fight 2020, an organization that promotes fair election processes in the state of Georgia and around the country. There are many more examples of groups who might have not succeeded in their outcome, but move forward with purposeful and meaningful work to create sustainable change for our communities. Engaging in leadership experiences requires a high-level of responsibility, which can be intimidating; particularly with the amount of concerning issues in our world. Also, there are systemic barriers to accessing leadership roles and therefore, members of under-represented groups do not have equal opportunities to engage in leadership. However, by witnessing others engage in the leadership process, we can identify strategies for our leadership self-efficacy development.

Failure is a real thing that we all experience, especially when working on teams or in groups to make something happen. What example do you have when you or a team/group failed at something you were trying to do? How did you or your team/group learn from that moment?

Opportunities. Reading about other people's leadership experiences and the tactics used to navigate challenges or opportunities is useful in our learning. Further, autobiographies and books about someone's life that does not explicitly claim to be leadership scholarship is an open window to consider how their story connects to leadership. We recommend to not only refer to your leadership section of your local bookstore or online, but encourage looking at sections like history, biography, poetry, social issues, short stories, psychology, or sociology. These sections can include a broader conceptualization of leadership, one not rooted in an individual's story, but one rooted in a collective experience for something greater than themselves. In addition, a critical consideration is that your efficacy beliefs do influence others, even if you do not have a book written about you. Your family members, friends, classmates, student organization members, and peers observe you engaging in the leadership process, much like you observe others. It is important to be open and share with people in your life by telling stories. Storytelling can be used as a tool for increasing leadership self-efficacy in others, particularly stories that reflect the ways you do not fit mainstream images of leadership, and how you have defied those boundaries of difference (Crosby, 2017).

Affirmation and Feedback on Leadership Experiences

It is valuable to desire real-world knowledge and skills and to use college as a time to do it. But those experiences need to be coupled with support and feedback while pursuing leadership learning. Affirmation and feedback on leadership experiences advance leadership self-efficacy because it encourages you to persevere, learn, celebrate, or adapt depending on your experience (Bandura, 1997). This feedback can come from various places—an advisor, professor, peer, mentor, supervisor, follower, and teammate—someone whom you work with often. Feedback should come from a place of care and love for the growth of the individual, as well as the group. For feedback to feel loving, especially critical feedback, there needs to be a relationship of trust built over time. Feedback can be received differently depending on the relationship and context within which it is given. Moreover, the individual receiving the feedback has a choice in deciding if what is given is accurate for them. Sometimes feedback may not be processed or accepted until much later in someone's life, but reflection is an active process that is done over time and is core to leadership learning.

Barriers. Finding faculty or staff members on campus who can advocate for you to seek opportunities, who know about processes of the institution, and who can build a relationship with you can be a challenge but a beneficial opportunity during college. We recommend finding advocates and key relationships who will be honest with you, hold you accountable, share opportunities, and process moments where you need them. However, as a cautionary consideration, the role of older adults as an area of sensemaking for leadership self-efficacy is overly stressed in leadership learning. This is not all together bad when mentorship relationships are treated as two-sided, but so often the flow of power goes one way which is detrimental to a learning relationship. For example, simply because someone is older, does not mean we should assume their advice or feedback holds more power than another. Further, simply because someone is in a position of authority does not mean their knowledge is certain. An overreliance on meaning-making from others can often result in a decreased belief in your voice and internal processing abilities. Belief can be influenced by validation, gained internally through a growth-based mindset, and impact how an individual feels about others and a community as a whole. We are all figuring out the complex process of working with others, which requires learning, practice, and reflection.

Opportunities. Since reflection is an active process, one strategy for this area of increasing leadership self-efficacy is to engage with other leaders on campus through taking a leadership course, engaging in a leadership program, getting involved in students organizations, and doing activism or community service work with other student leaders (Kodama & Laylo, 2017; Komives et al., 2005; Owen et al., 2017; Turman et al., 2018). In particular, Kodama and Laylo (2017), describe how identity-based student organizations (i.e., groups organized around shared marginalized social identities) are crucial for developing leadership self-efficacy because it merges identity and leadership development. A story shared by Kodama and Laylo (2017) included a student involved in an organization for undocumented students. This student explained how important the support, advice, and encouragement they received from their group members increased their belief in their ability to address lobbyists and government officials. Talking through strategies, clarifying their rights, and connecting with their peers helped this student feel empowered to act and create change for their community (Kodama & Laylo, 2017).

> Consider a time, either in a friend group, student organization, or a class group project, where feedback was not discussed and it could have improved the experience. What would have changed if "Feedback = Love" was a belief your group agreed on? What could you have done to create an environment where feedback was valued and important to your group? Use included Table 4.2 for your reflections.

Internal Thoughts and Feelings on Leadership Experiences

The last source Bandura (1997) describes as a source of efficacy is physiological and affective states. You may have the knowledge and skills necessary to move towards solving a problem or creating change in your community; however, your internal thoughts influence the likelihood of you taking action (Dugan & Komives, 2010).

Barriers. Our internal thoughts and feelings are significantly influenced by our external environment in college, and we often do not rely on our internal processing until much later in our lives (Baxter Magolda, 2008). Strategies for building greater leadership self-efficacy would be increasing your knowledge of identity development, how you or your group have

Table 4.2

Affirmation and Feedback Reflection

Group, Organization, or Project	Nature of Feedback (i.e., none, one-sided, negative, honest, etc.)	What would have changed with a "Feedback = Love" belief?	What action steps could I have taken?
ex: Event Planning Team	One-sided; only the chair of the event gave feedback to the group. Felt controlling and like they did not trust us.	Could have established a relationship and clear purpose for the group. Would have felt like the chair trusted us and we could give them feedback too.	Encouraged an open discussion; discussed my strengths and where I felt I could contribute most.

been affected by external environments/systems and engaging in spiritual perspective-taking. Over time, similar to our experiences, you may have internalized negative messaging about your abilities because of social identity assumptions or stereotype threat (Williams, 2016). These messages are developed to maintain a specific social order, or institutionalized oppression, and perpetuated through a range of venues, like the media, education, government, and more. Often subconsciously absorbed, without a critical awareness, it can cause negative or belittling beliefs which limit engagement in the leadership process (Williams, 2016).

Opportunities. As described in the next chapter, a goal to address these internal thoughts would be to develop critical hope and critical consciousness (Freire, 1970), which "allows individuals to live their lives in a hopeful, yet critical way, despite the institutionally oppressive system that surrounds them" (Williams, 2016, p. 92). To be able to do this you may need to increase your understanding of systems of oppression, how being socialized within these systems result in certain beliefs or behaviors, and being aware of your own identities. This acknowledgment and increase of critical consciousness directly relate to an increased ability to reject negative messaging. This strategy can also encourage our motivation to engage in leadership (Bertrand Jones et al., 2016). Mindfulness and reflection take time—time that we often do not commit to—but critical consciousness requires introspection (Williams, 2016). Introspection can feel very different from the tasks that are required of you in student organizations and through your academic coursework. However, prioritizing self-care, well-being, and purposeful reflection are all elements of spiritual perspective-taking. Think about times where you have been on a retreat of some kind and ask yourself—was this "retreat" time to be mindful and focus on the purpose of this experience or was it to organize tasks and plan the experience? Even times created to center reflection and spiritual perspective-taking (i.e., retreats) are overwhelmed with tasks and planning. A better strategy is to create a habit or practice of reflection, grounded in encouraging growth and introspection.

PERSONAL REFLECTION

- Consider a time where you felt you were engaging positively with others to create meaningful change or completing a complex task. How did your perceptions of what you believe you excelled at differ from what others perceived you excelled at?

   o In what ways does this relate to your leadership self-efficacy beliefs?
- How do historical social justice movements influence current empowerment and mobilization efforts to create change, both in your individual life and in the community or society broadly?
- After reviewing each of the leadership self-efficacy sources, what sources do you feel most comfortable with or enact frequently? What sources would you be interested in exploring more in practice?

DISCUSSION QUESTIONS

- Explain in your own words how efficacy relates to capacity and identity.
- In what ways could increasing critical consciousness influence leadership capacity and identity, as described in this book? What about engaging in spiritual perspective-taking?
- Consider your daily routine or activities you engage with frequently—how can you center leadership learning more intentionally in your life?

TAKING LEADERSHIP EFFICACY FURTHER

Activity #1: Leadership Timeline

Create a timeline of how your beliefs about leadership have shifted throughout your life. Start from the first moment you remember learning about leadership or what a leader was. Consider moments where you identified as a leader or understood your own definition of leadership. Brainstorm experiences, moments, and people who influenced your leadership learning. Be as creative as you would like. Once completed, grab pencils, highlighters, markers, pens, or crayons of different colors (make sure you have at least 4 different colors). Review your completed timeline focused on the 4 efficacy sources. Shade/mark (with a different color for each source) at least one moment, experience, or person related to each efficacy source.

Efficacy Sources	Color on Timeline	How did this moment, experience, or person shape your leadership self-efficacy beliefs?
Direct or Mastery Experiences *Your/Our Leadership Experiences* • Experiences that promote collaboration, leadership learning, and skill development		
Vicarious Experience *Witnessing Other Leadership Experiences* • Observation of others engaging in the leadership process, with or without a formal title/role		
Verbal Persuasion and Affirmation *Affirmation and Feedback on Leadership Experiences* • Receiving encouragement, affirmation, and feedback from others' (mentors, friends, teammates, teachers, advisors, etc.)		
Assessment of Physiological and Affective States *Internal Thoughts and Feelings on Leadership Experiences* • Understanding your/our moods, feelings, energy, and stress levels in relation to engaging in the leadership process		

After you have done the entire activity, respond to these reflection questions:

- How have you thought about and experienced leadership differently depending on the context?
- How have your influential experiences, moments, and people in your life shaped your leadership self-efficacy?
- What new reflections are present after learning about leadership self-efficacy as a concept?

Activity #2: Efficacy in Stories

Reading and sharing stories can assist us with understanding efficacy in more tangible ways. This activity requests you to select a story and analyze how it reflects efficacy beliefs. The story can come from sharing a personal narrative, researching a historical account, reading a biography, or a description of a current event. Once you have found a story to analyze, review the below definitions of efficacy pulled from the chapter and consider how the story reflects various efficacy beliefs.

Concept and Source	Adapted Definition
Efficacy (Bandura, 1997)	Belief in one's ability to successfully accomplish a specific task in a particular context
Leadership Efficacy (Dugan, 2017; Hannah et al., 2008)	Belief in one's ability to successfully engage in collective groups and in the leadership process beyond specific roles
Leader Efficacy (Dugan, 2017; Hannah et al., 2008)	Belief in one's abilities to successfully lead groups or teams through various positional roles and demands
Collective Efficacy (Hannah et al., 2008)	Shared belief in collective capabilities to organize and engage in the leadership process to accomplish goals or intended change

Journal or process with someone how the efficacy beliefs observed relate to your own beliefs, respond to these reflection questions:

- How might social location relate to these observations or your own beliefs?
- How do your beliefs affect your sense of self and engagement in the leadership process?
- What strategies could you use from this chapter to develop your efficacy?

CHAPTER 5

ENGAGEMENT

How Do I Continue to Grow?

Building off our reflection of identity, capacity, and efficacy we must also explore and learn about integrating these concepts when considering leadership as a process. This chapter explores integrating identity, capacity and, efficacy in how you engage in the process of leadership. The chapter also explains the culturally relevant leadership learning model and the five domains. As we move through this chapter consider the following questions:

- What is the relationship between your own identity, capacity, and efficacy?
- How do you consider leadership as a process from a growth mindset lens?
- How do you consider leadership as a process from a critical hope framework?
- How do you continue to grow as a leader and engage in leadership as a process?

Engaging in the Leadership Process:
Identity, Capacity, and Efficacy for College Students, pp. 65–77
Copyright © 2021 by Information Age Publishing
All rights of reproduction in any form reserved.

INTEGRATION OF IDENTITY, CAPACITY, AND EFFICACY

Through this book we have explored how engaging in the leadership process is rooted in one's identity, capacity, and efficacy (Guthrie et al., 2016). Chapter 2 addressed how the leadership process centers identity as being socially constructed and grounded in historical, political, and cultural forces (Jones, 2016). Chapter 3 highlighted how capacity is the integration of students' knowledge, attitudes, and skills, collectively reflecting their overall ability to engage in the leadership process (Dugan, 2017). Chapter 4 explored how efficacy is the expectation of success in specific activities; the belief you can successfully engage in group processes to reach common goals (Bandura, 1997). As Reichard and Walker (2016) stated, identity, capacity, and efficacy are interconnected and motivate individuals to engage in the leadership process. As we engage in leadership, our identity, capacity, and efficacy are enhanced - further motivating more engagement in leadership processes and working towards collective goals (Guthrie et al., 2016). Figure 5.1 reminds us of how we individually engage in the leadership process.

Figure 5.1

Individual Engaging in the Leadership Process

Adapted from Bertrand Jones, Guthrie, & Osteen, 2016

As the first chapter highlighted, culturally relevant leadership learning (CRLL) is a relatively new framework for understanding leadership learning. According to Bertrand Jones and colleagues (2016), the CRLL model seeks to "challenge old paradigms of leadership and learning, in order to consider new ways to educate students and develop leaders capable of challenging inequity to create social change" (p. 10). The model acknowledges the prevalence of all forms of oppression, such as racism, classism, and sexism. Culturally relevant leadership learning recognizes the concept and influence of power (Bertrand Jones et al., 2016). The model centers the individual engaged in the leadership process and the intersecting identities the individual holds. It acknowledges power in leadership, language, and campus climate; as well as power's sway on a leader and their ability to produce social change.

Regarding the power of language and words, CRLL acknowledges the importance of how certain words are defined or described, particularly the words leader and leadership. As chapter 1 addressed, not everyone defines these words the same. Social and cultural norms and ideologies have influenced what these terms mean to people from various backgrounds (Bertrand Jones et al., 2016). It is important to remember and understand this when considering your own leadership experiences in college. Leadership learning does not occur in a bubble, especially on college campuses that are microcosms of a greater society. The interaction between the student and the leadership process is encompassed by the campus climate and those experiencing the campus climate (Bertrand Jones et al., 2016).

As you remember from chapter 1, this environment, or campus climate, is inclusive of five domains. The domains are: (a) historical legacy of inclusion/exclusion, (b) compositional diversity, (c) psychological dimension, (d) behavioral dimension, and (e) organizational/structural dimension (Bertrand Jones et al., 2016). The historical legacy of inclusion/exclusion domain acknowledges that People of Color have historically been left out of the leadership conversation. It also examines who has been traditionally marginalized or underrepresented when it comes to leadership in a particular environment. Compositional diversity refers to the numerical representation of diverse populations of student. In other words, who is present? The psychological dimension consists of the internal processes individuals use to understand and make meaning of their realities and concepts like diversity, equity, and inclusion. The behavioral dimension examines the interactions between students—paying particular attention to the quality of those exchanges; how do students treat each other based on difference or perceived differences. Organization and structural dimensions attend to the frameworks and processes in place that guide the day-to-day decision-making of the institutions; what policies, practices, and organizational characteristics keep some groups perpetually marginalized. The CRLL model stresses that a student engaging in the leadership process and how one's identities are experienced, must account for the environment and context.

As you continue your leadership learning journey, let us revisit this metaphor of traveling in a car. The road is not always easy, there will be potholes, bumps, and roadblocks, but there will also be sunny days with no traffic and music playing as well. These conditions and essentially the environment in which you are traveling are the domains just discussed. Your environment needs to be considered as you navigate the terrain of your leadership learning journey. In this metaphor, let us think about you, as the individual driving. You have the ability to steer your learning in various directions. The steering wheel of the leadership learning framework supports you taking control of your journey. Your way of being in the process of leadership, your understanding of how you engage, is your identity, capacity, and efficacy.

Throughout this book, we have provided specific language for centering identity, capacity, and efficacy when engaging in the leadership process, with the ultimate goal of moving towards social change. Leadership learning can be messy, and there is no map or blueprint of how to do it that totally predicts the challenges you might experience along the way. We also acknowledge the realities engaging in leadership does not always feel empowering and exciting because there are systems of historical legacy of inclusion/exclusion at play. Engaging in the leadership process can also take an emotional toll on you because of the passion and devotion needed to work towards positive change. Remember to constantly be thinking through your own agency and offer yourself and others compassion, love, and validation (Osteen et al., 2016). Throughout this book we have intentionally moved between self (I) and collective (we/group) while thinking about experiences, hopes, challenges, and opportunities to grow our own leader identity, capacity, and efficacy.

CULTURALLY RELEVANT LEADERSHIP LEARNING AND IDENTITY

At the center of the CRLL model is a three-part synthesis of development that the individual engages (Bertrand Jones et al., 2016). The CRLL model is centered on the development of three aspects: identity, capacity, and efficacy (see Figure 5.1). The first piece is the individual—the person who is being developed. Leadership learning is happening all around you and you cannot disconnect who you are from what you are experiencing, nor should you. Leadership learning "recognize[s] how individuals' identity and their intersections with power and privilege reciprocally influence the context" (Osteen et al., 2016, p. 102) of leadership on their campus. When we continue to explore and make meaning of our own identities, we must also be constantly considering the role of the identities of others in the compositional diversity and the history of inclusion/exclusion of our peers and the groups they are a part of. What about the organizational structures and who holds or has historically held positions? Again, reiterating your agency and collective ability to hold institutions accountable. If there continues to be policies and practices that perpetually keep some groups marginalized you have agency to address these inequities. Considering CRLL, this alignment might also be rooted in a student's own personal identities and understandings of those identities.

CULTURALLY RELEVANT LEADERSHIP LEARNING AND CAPACITY

The second aspect CRLL is centered around is the individual's capacity for engaging in the leadership process. As Chapter 3 highlighted, the skills of leadership can and should be learned and leadership capacities are interconnected and with one's knowledge, skills, and experiences. When engaging in the leadership process and honoring one's past knowledge and experiences, we have to remember the knowledge of leadership is complex and nuanced. We have to continuously be building our capacity to deconstruct the leadership process (Osteen et al., 2016; Owen et al., 2017). Deconstructing leadership allows for critical examination of the process and addressing challenges that will occur. Deconstructing in leadership also allows for a reframing of situations that we at first might see as problems but can be reframed as challenges that can be addressed as a part of the leadership process. By gaining new skills and experiences one's capacity for leadership continues to grow. Having a sense of self-awareness, being willing to embrace vulnerability, and actively learning across difference are other ways to continue growing your capacity for leadership (Osteen et al., 2016). Additionally, group awareness is also an important skill to continue to develop when engaging in the leadership process and building capacity.

When understanding how capacity and culturally relevant leadership learning are integrated, consider how one learns the skills of leadership, or how to act on the understandings gained about leadership. As you grow in your capacity for leadership, reflect on ways to use these skills and knowledge to work towards positive social change. An approach to culturally relevant leadership learning and capacity, acknowledges how leadership can be rooted in power and privilege for an individual or collective group and how some skills and abilities for one group can be prioritized as "good leadership" and minimized for another group or individual. That is why leaders must also build their capacity for leadership to include strategies to negotiate and create collective change that addresses injustices and inequities at all levels (Owen et al., 2017).

CULTURALLY RELEVANT LEADERSHIP
LEARNING AND EFFICACY

As discussed in Chapter 4, simply being in a leadership role does not mean that you have developed your leadership efficacy. Learning and development should be the primary focus of leadership self-efficacy, this transitions the notion of positionality and outcome to collaboration and process (Murphy & Johnson, 2016). Influenced by Murphy and Johnson (2016) and Machida-Kosuga (2017) we offer a consideration of focusing on *leadership learning efficacy*. Murphy and Johnson (2016) described a concept called leader-developmental efficacy, which focuses on the belief about one's ability to change or develop their leadership skills. They describe how people with high leader-developmental efficacy will engage in more leadership development activities to grow and develop over time. Machida-Kosuga (2017) described how learning self-efficacy is important for developing leadership competencies and encouraged a learning orientation for students. In his original work, Bandura (1997) also asserts that learning self-efficacy is critical for one's development. It allows people to engage in adaptive thoughts and behavioral processes that facilitate their persistence (Bandura & Locke, 2003).

Merging these two bodies of work is the foundation for the focus on leadership learning efficacy. Leadership learning is defined as, "changes in knowledge, skills, behavior, attitudes, and values resulting from educational experiences, both co-curricular and curricular in nature, associated with the activity of leadership" (Guthrie & Jenkins, 2018, p. 57). Leadership learning efficacy includes beliefs about your or the group's ability to develop or change knowledge, skills, behavior, attitudes, and values associated with the activity of leadership. Put simply, it is a belief about one's ability to learn about leadership and apply it to one's life. This would require leadership learning, rooted in critical consciousness, to be centered in your educational, organizational, and community engagement experiences, but not disconnected from your identity and capacity. You (and group members) are active participants in your leadership learning and your commitment to learning can contribute to your leadership self-efficacy beliefs. Aligned with CRLL, it is crucial to understand leadership as ordinary people who do extraordinary things with others (Osteen et al., 2016).

Now that you have learned about the leadership process and the integration of identity, capacity, and efficacy, how does understanding the leadership process now inform your approach to leadership and being a leader?

FUTURE DIRECTIONS

When integrating identity, capacity, and efficacy but also engaging in the leadership process, consider the concepts of growth mindset and critical hope. Critical hope provides a way forward. Within this framework, critique and hopefulness cannot be separated and as a leader you need both. Leaders need to be able to critique the world as it is, while holding on to hope for a different future rooted in social change (Freire, 1992). With growth mindset, leaders believe their capacity can be developed through gaining meaningful experiences, developing good strategies, and incorporating feedback from others. Leaders tend to achieve more than those with a more fixed mindset (those who believe their talents are innate gifts). This is because they worry less about looking smart and they put more energy into learning (Dweck, 2006, 2016).

The Difference Between Fixed Mindset and Growth Mindset

Having a fixed mindset creates an urgency to prove yourself over and over. With a fixed mindset, leaders see criticism as an attack on their character, and avoid criticism because they feel they are being called a "bad leader" when being criticized. Well known Stanford Professor of Psychology, Carol Dweck (2006), introduced the concept of fixed mindset and highlights that it centers on this belief that you can learn new things, but you cannot really change who you are; fixed mindset also applies to one's character, meaning you are a certain kind of person with specific character qualities, and there is not much that can be done to drastically change qualities (Dweck, 2006). In a fixed mindset, leaders believe their basic abilities, their intelligence, their talents, are just fixed traits. They have a certain amount and that's that, and then their goal becomes to look smart all the time and never appear as though they do not have the answers. Fixed mindset can also be a collective thought for those engaged in the leadership process and limit ideas and possibilities for making collective change.

Growth mindset centers on the belief that no matter how much intelligence you have, you can always increase your intelligence or your character qualities, no matter what type of person you are, you can always change and grow as a person (Dweck, 2006). The hallmark of growth mindset is a passion for sticking with it, especially when things are not going well (Dweck, 2006; Dweck, 2016). Additionally, Dweck's (2006) growth mindset is really about your approach to challenges, effort, and feedback that embraces the process necessary to make a personal change. For example, leaders who welcome challenges to the group or change process and see setbacks as necessary, believe they can learn and grow from those experiences. They even view failure as additional feedback to improve rather than an indication of self-worth. Having a growth mindset encourages learning and effort. Having a collective growth mindset is also important for all those engaged in the leadership process. If a group truly believes they can improve something, they will be much more driven to learn new things and engage in the leadership process. With a growth mindset, criticism is seen as valuable feedback and should be openly embraced by both the individual and the collective group. When feedback is constructive and meant to better a person or the leadership process, feedback does equal love (Guthrie & Jenkins, 2018), and can make a positive impact to all engaged in the leadership process together (see Table 5.2).

Now that you have learned the difference between a fixed mindset and a growth mindset, do you have examples of when you have seen a growth and a fixed mindset from a leader when you were engaged in the leadership process? In what ways can you continue to grow your growth mindset when engaged in the leadership process?

Critical Hope

Hope can seem like a lofty optimistic mindset, a way of being and a goal to strive for, but we cannot hope without critiquing the present context and imagining a different world. We cannot truly hope unless we embody hope in our lived experiences and our approach to leadership by naming the problem, developing a solution, enacting it, reflecting, modifying, and trying again in a constant cycle of transformation (Bozalek et al., 2015; Freire, 1992). Within a critical hope framework, we propose that you as a leader engage in understanding history with a critical lens, not be afraid of using your imagination for envisioning a different way forward, and provide space for practical steps to execute the vision (Bozalek et al., 2015; Freire, 1992). To this we encourage you to distinguish between critical hope, naïve hope, and false hope. Naïve hope is optimism without a sense of personal responsibility. Naïve hope is expecting that things will turn out alright even if one puts forth no effort to make it so. False hope is the idea that working hard will result in one succeeding no matter what, without critiquing the systems or context that limit some being successful with no effort, while others not being successful with full effort (Bozalek et al., 2015).

Cultivating critical hope starts with leaders navigating systems with a dual lens of attempting to contribute to positive social change while also being realistic about the painful realities of the world and still seeing the possibilities for progress (Bishundat, 2018). This is important work, but it also comes at a toll for leaders. Critical hope provides a resource to stay in

Table 5.2

Differences Between Fixed Mindset and Growth Mindset

Fixed Mindset	Growth Mindset	Things to Consider
Not everyone is a good leader, just do your best.	When you learn a new approach to leadership, it grows your leadership capacity and efficacy.	Settling for doing your best, without adjusting or learning new approaches to leadership is fixed and not rooted in growth.
That's ok, maybe leadership is just not one of your strengths.	If you catch yourself saying, "I'm just not a leader," add the word 'yet' to the end of the sentence.	Fixed mindset doesn't allow for the possibility for growth and it limits both the leader's capacity and efficacy to engage in the leadership process.
Don't worry, you'll get it if you keep trying.	Keep trying, but adjust your strategy and approach each time to meet the needs of others and also consider the context of the situation.	If leaders are using the wrong strategies, their efforts might not work. Also, you might feel like you failed if your approach continues to not be successful.
Great effort, you tried your best.	The point is not to be a perfect leader right away. The point is to engage in the leadership process and learn along the way. How can you learn and grow from each experience?	Leaders must do more than try their best. A leaders best always has room to grow and be willing to accept critical feedback that can aide in their growth.

Adapted from Carol Dweck (2006).

these challenges in ways that are healthy and sustainable (Bozalek et al., 2014; Dugan, 2017; Preskill & Brookfield, 2009). Since leaders play key roles in supporting, developing, and nurturing the leadership capacities of others, leaders must cultivate critical hope in their own lives, so they are better prepared to do so in the lives of those they are engaged in leadership with. Leadership for social change requires individuals to collectively engage with one another in an ongoing struggle for justice and equity (Chunoo et al., 2019; Dugan, 2017; Ospina et al., 2012). As you take on these challenges, cultivating critical hope is essential to engaging in the leadership process.

A key aspect of leadership is one's responsibility to be in service to others and work within a collective toward addressing social concerns (Komives et al., 2006). A tool that might be useful to leaders engaged in the leadership process is the cycle of liberation (Harro, 2000). In Chapter 2, we introduced the cycle of socialization, which helps us understand how we are socialized to play certain roles, how we are affected by issues of oppression, and how we as individuals and collectively as a society maintain a system based on power (Harro, 2000). The cycle of liberation is the process in which people come to a deeper understanding of how injustices are perpetuated and what the individual's role is in this systemic process (Harro, 2000). The person with a new deeper understanding then seeks new paths for creating social change and taking themselves and the group or society at large towards empowerment or liberation. Social issues that impact our communities are not easily fixed overnight and require a high-level of emotional endurance and stamina. As a result, critical hope allows leaders to support the work of the collective and contribute to a process with the understanding that individuals may see limited to no progress toward resolving these issues within their lifetime, but they will still press on for the greater good, even if the outcomes are in the distant future.

What does critical hope look and feel like for your own leadership identity, capacity, and efficacy? How does critical hope play a role in the world you would like to see? What role do leaders play in having critical hope for addressing inequities in the world?

TYING IT ALL TOGETHER

Throughout this book we have centered identity, capacity, and efficacy when considering engaging in the leadership process. None of these concepts are fixed. There are opportunities for growth and deeper reflection for each of these in our lives and each time we engage in the leadership process with others. Our experiences and environment definitely impact our understandings of identity, capacity, and efficacy. Remember the goal should always be growth for the purpose of being the best leader you can be. Leadership should have purpose and encourage hope to move towards positive change, no matter the context. It is important to reflect on our identities and how we understand ourselves as leaders in relation to our privileges and marginalized identities. Opportunities to gain experience, develop skills, and grow our capacity for leadership prepares us for the moments in the leadership process that are challenging and discouraging. Remember that efficacy is about agency and a certainty that you have the abilities within yourself to engage in the leadership process and impact change. Efficacy is also rooted in a belief in yourself that there are always opportunities to grow and learn from new experiences. Efficacy is at the root of human agency (Bandura, 1997; Hannah et al., 2008); meaning by understanding the details and sources of our beliefs, we can act, adapt, or change. In tying this together, we are all on a leadership learning journey for the betterment of not only ourselves, but the world we live in. We have been and continued to be socialized in various ways, so our values and beliefs are instilled in us and prepares us to act certain ways. Individually we need to reflect and be critical of how our identity, capacity, and efficacy influence not only our leadership learning journey, but in how we engage in the leadership process with others. It matters. You matter.

PERSONAL REFLECTION

- How does your personal identity, capacity, and efficacy determine how you engage in the leadership process? What role does each play for you?
- What do you think are the most important distinctions between a fixed mindset and a growth mindset?
- What approaches to a growth mindset do you need to work on developing?
- What is the biggest personal barrier you face in developing critical hope when engaging in the leadership process?

DISCUSSION QUESTIONS

- In organizations or groups you are a member of, how does leadership identity, capacity, and efficacy show up in relation to yours and others engagement in the leadership process?
  - o How can we foster a collective identity, capacity, and efficacy of leaders and followers among equals?
- How does a growth mindset support culturally relevant leadership learning?
- How does critical hope support culturally relevant leadership learning?
- What do you think your responsibility is, as a leader, to acknowledge identity, capacity, and efficacy in others?

TAKING LEADERSHIP FURTHER

Activity #1: Fixed Mindset Versus Growth Mindset Leadership Plan

Think about your own leadership identity, capacity, and efficacy and what aspects are fixed and how they can be more rooted in a growth mindset. Then develop a plan to change these fixed leadership approaches into long-term growth mindset leadership approaches.

Fixed Mindset	Growth	Short-Term (6 months)	Longer-Term (1–2 years)
ex: Not being a "Good Leader"	*Always striving to be a better leader*	*I will start seeking feedback from those engaged in the leadership process with me about ways I can be a better leader or follower.*	*Over the next year, I will continue to apply feedback I receive after engaging in the leadership process. I will consider the feedback in terms of my leadership identity, capacity, and efficacy.*

Activity #2: Critical Hope and the Cycle of Liberation

Adapted from Cycle of Liberation (Harro, 2000)

Think about a social issue or injustice you would like to address. This can be within organizations you are involved, or in your local community, or more broad social issues in society. Consider the process of liberation below when working towards change. To enter the cycle there is usually a critical incident or some awareness or a "waking up" moment. What would this cycle look like for you? For example, what is at your "core" How are you getting ready and what does it look like to reach out to build community? What will creating change produce?

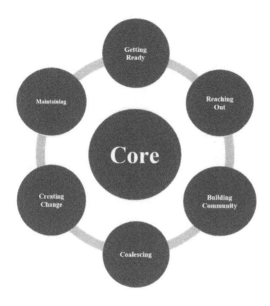

Cycle of Liberation	Explanation	What does this look like for you when engaging in the leadership process for the purpose of making change?
CORE	Self-Love, Self-Efficacy, Self-Balance, Joy, Support	
GETTING READY	Empowerment of self, consciousness raising, gaining inspiration and purpose	
REACHING OUT	Moving from focusing on self to centering others, speaking out/naming injustices	
BUILDING COMMUNITY	Working with others, questioning assumptions about others	
COALESCING	Organizing strategically, developing an action plan to move towards change	
CREATING CHANGE	Transforming institutions and organizing to create a new culture	
MAINTAINING	Spreading hope and inspiration, centering self-care and supporting others	

REFERENCES

Abes, E. S., Jones, S. R., & McEwen, M. K. (2007). Reconceptualizing the model of multiple dimensions of identity: The role of meaning-making capacity in the construction of multiple identities. *Journal of College Student Development, 48*(1), 1–22. https://doi.org/10.1353/csd.2007.0000

Ayman, R., Adams, S., Fisher, B., & Hartmen, E. (2003). Leadership development in higher education institutions: A present and future perspective. In S. E. Murphy & R. E. Riggio (Eds.), *The future of leadership development* (pp. 201–222). Lawrence Erlbaum.

Astin, H. S., & Astin, A. W. (1996). *A social change model of leadership development guidebook. Version III*. UCLA Higher Education Research Institute.

Bandura, A. (1997). *Self-efficacy: The exercise of control*. W. H. Freeman.

Bandura, A., & Locke, E. A. (2003). Negative self–efficacy effects revisited. *Journal of Applied Psychology, 88*, 87–89.

Baxter Magolda, M. B. (2008). Three elements of self–authorship. *Journal of College Student Development, 49*(4), 269–284.

Bertrand Jones, T., Guthrie, K. L., & Osteen, L. (2016). Critical domains of culturally relevant leadership learning: A call to transform leadership programs. In K. L. Guthrie, T. Bertrand Jones, & L. Osteen (Eds.), *New Directions for Student Leadership: No. 152. Developing culturally relevant leadership learning* (pp. 9–21). Jossey-Bass.

Birkelund, R. (2000). Ethics and education. *Nursing Ethics, 7*(6), 473–480.

Bishundat, D., Velazquez Phillip, D., & Gore, W. (2018). Cultivating critical hope: The too often forgotten dimension of critical leadership development. In J. P. Dugan (Ed.), *New Directions for Student Leadership: No. 159. Integrating Critical Perspectives into Leadership Development* (pp. 91–102). Jossey-Bass.

Bolden, R., & Gosling, J. (2006). Leadership competencies: Time to change the tune? *Leadership, 2*(2), 147–163.

Bozalek, V. G., Mcmillan, W., Marshall, D. E., November, M., Daniels, A., & Sylvester, T. (2014). Analyzing the professional development of teaching and learning from a political ethics of care perspective. *Teaching in Higher Education*, 1–12. Taylor & Francis. https://doi.org/10.1080/13562517.2014.880681

Brungardt, C. L. (1998). The new fact of leadership: Implications for training educational leaders. *On the Horizon, 6*(1), 7–8.

Burkhardt, J. C., & Zimmerman–Oster, K. (1999). How does the richest, most widely educated nation prepare leaders for its future? *Proteus, 16*(2), 9.

Burns, J. M. (1978). *Leadership*. Harper & Row.

Carlyle, T. (1888). *On heroes, hero-worship and the heroic in history*. Fredrick A. Stokes & Brother.

Chunoo, V. S., Beatty, C. C., Gruver, M. D. (2019). Leadership educator as social justice educator. In K. L. Priest & D. M. Jenkins (Eds.), *New Directions for Student Leadership: No. 164. Becoming and Being a Leadership Educator* (pp. 87–103). Jossey-Bass.

Conger, J. A., & Ready, D. A. (2004). Rethinking leadership competencies. *Leader to Leader, 32*, 41–47.

Crosby, B. C. (2017). *Teaching leadership: An integrative approach*. Routledge.

Davis, T., & Harrison, L. M. (2013). *Advancing social justice: Tools, pedagogies, and strategies to transform your campus*. Jossey-Bass.

Denzine, G. (1999). Personal and collective efficacy: Essential components of college students' leadership development. *Concepts & Connections, 8*(1), 1–5.

Dugan, J. P. (2017). *Leadership theory: Cultivating critical perspectives*. Jossey-Bass.

Dugan, J. P., Garland, J. L., Jacoby, B., & Gasiorski, A. (2008). Understanding commuter student self–efficacy for leadership: A within-group analysis. *NASPA Journal, 45*(2), 282–310.

Dugan, J. P., Kodama, C., Correia, B., & Associates. (2013). *Multi–Institutional Study of Leadership insight report: Leadership program delivery*. National Clearinghouse for Leadership Programs.

Dugan, J. P., & Komives, S. R. (2010). Influences on college students' capacity for socially responsible leadership. *Journal of College Student Development, 51*, 525–549.

Dugan, J. P., & Komives, S. R. (2011). Leadership theories. In S. R. Komives, J. P. Dugan, J. E. Owen, C. Slack, W. Wagner, and Associates (Eds.), *The handbook of student leadership development* (2nd ed., pp. 35–58). Jossey-Bass.

Dweck, C. (2006). *Mindset: The new psychology of success*. Random House.

Dweck, C. (2016). What having a "Growth Mindset" actually means. *Harvard Business Review*. https://hbr.org/2016/01/what-having-a-growth-mindset-actually-means

Freire, P. (1970). *Pedagogy of the oppressed*. Continuum.

Freire, P. (1992) *Pedagogy of hope—Reliving pedagogy of the oppressed*. Continuum.

Fryberg, S. A., & Stephens, N. M. (2010). When the world is colorblind, American Indians are invisible: A diversity science approach. *Psychological Inquiry, 21*, 115–119.

Goddard, R. D., Hoy, W. K., & Woolfolk Hoy, A. (2004). Collective efficacy beliefs: Theoretical development, empirical evidence, and future directions. *Educational Researcher, 33*(3), 3–13.

Goleman, D. (1998). What makes a leader? *Harvard Business Review, 76,* 92–105.

Guthrie, K. L., Bertrand Jones, T., Osteen, L. (Eds.). (2016). *New Directions for Student Leadership: No. 152. Developing culturally relevant leadership learning.* Jossey-Bass.

Guthrie, K. L., Bertrand Jones, T., Osteen, L., & Hu, S. (2013). Cultivating leader identity and capacity in students from diverse backgrounds. *ASHE Higher Education Report, 39*(4). Jossey-Bass.

Guthrie, K. L., & Jenkins, D. M. (2018). *The role of leadership educators: Transforming learning.* Information Age Publishing.

Hannah, S. T., Avolio, B. J., Lutans, F., & Harms, P. D. (2008). Leadership efficacy: Review and future directions. *Leadership Quarterly, 19,* 669–692.

Harro, B. (2000). The cycle of liberation. In M. A. Adams, W. J. Blumenfeld, R. Castaneda, H. W. Hackman, M. L. Peters, & X. Zuniga (Eds.), *Readings for diversity and social justice* (pp. 463–469). Routledge.

Harvey, M., & Riggio, R. E. (Eds.). (2011). *Leadership studies: The dialogue of disciplines.* Edward Elgar.

Irwin, T. (1999). *Aristotle: Nicomachean ethics.* Hackett.

Jones, S. R. (2016). Authenticity in leadership: Intersectionality of identities. In K. L. Guthrie, T. B. Jones, & L. Osteen (Eds.), *New directions for higher education, no. 152. Developing culturally relevant leadership learning* (pp. 23–34). Jossey-Bass.

Jones, S. R. & McEwen, M. K. (2000). A conceptual model of multiple dimensions of identity. *Journal of College Student Development, 41,* 405–414.

Jones, S. R., Torres, V., & Arminio, J. (2013). *Negotiating the complexities of qualitative research in higher education: Fundamental elements and issues* (2nd ed.). Routledge.

Jones, S. R., & Abes, E. S. (2013). *Identity development of college students: Advancing frameworks for multiple dimensions of identity.* Jossey-Bass.

Josselson, R. (1996). On writing other people's lives: Self–analytic reflections of a narrative researcher. In R. Josselson (Ed.), *The narrative study of lives, Vol. 4. Ethics and process in the narrative study of lives* (pp. 60–71). SAGE.

Katz, R. L. (1955). Skills of an effective administrator. *Harvard Business Review, 33*(1), 33–42

Kellerman, B. (2012). Cut off at the pass: The limits of leadership in the 21st century. *Governance Studies at Brookings Institution,* 1–11. https://www.brookings.edu/wp–content/uploads/2016/06/0810_leadership_deficit_kellerman.pdf

Kodama, C., & Dugan, J. P. (2013). Leveraging leadership efficacy in college students: Disaggregating data to examine unique predictors by race. *Equity & Excellence in Education, 46,* 184–201.

Kodama, C. M., & Laylo, R. (2017). The unique context of identity–based student organizations in development leadership. In D. M. Rosch (Ed.), *New Directions for Student Leadership: No. 155. The role of student organizations in developing leadership* (pp. 71–81). Jossey-Bass.

Kotter, J. (1990). *A force for change: How leadership differs from management.* Free Press.

Komives, S. R., Lucas, N., & McMahon, T. R. (1998). *Exploring leadership: For college students who want to make a difference.* Jossey-Bass.

Komives, S. R., Lucas, N., & McMahon, T. R. (2013). *Exploring leadership: For college students who want to make a difference* (3rd ed.). Jossey-Bass.

Komives, S. R., Owen, J. E., Longerbeam, S. D., Mainella, F. C., & Osteen, L. (2005). Developing a leadership identity: A grounded theory. *Journal of College Student Development, 46*(6), 593–611.

Komives, S. R., Longerbeam, S. D., Owen, J. E., Mainella, F. C., & Osteen, L. (2006). A leadership identity development model: Applications from a grounded theory. *Journal of College Student Development, 47,* 401–418.

Kouzes, J. M., & Posner, B. Z. (2012). *The leadership challenge: How to make extraordinary things happen in organizations* (5th ed.). Jossey-Bass.

Kouzes, J. M., & Posner, B. Z. (2017). *Our authors' research.* Retrieved from http://www.leadershipchallenge.com/research-section-our-authors-research.aspx

Kouzes, J. M., & Posner, B. Z. (2018). *Student leadership challenge* (3rd ed.). Jossey-Bass.

Krauss, S. E., & Hamid, J. A. (2015). Exploring the relationship between campus leadership development and undergraduate student motivation to lead among a Malaysian sample. *Journal of Further and Higher Education, 39*(1), 1–26.

Kynard, C. (2013). *Vernacular insurrections: Race, Black protest, and the new century in composition-literacies studies.* State University of New York Press.

Machida–Kosuga, M. (2017). The interaction of efficacy and leadership competency development. In C. Seemiller (Ed.), *New Directions for Student Leadership: No. 156. A competency-based approach for student leadership development* (pp. 19–30). Jossey-Bass.

Machida, M., & Schaubroeck, J. (2011). The role of self–efficacy beliefs in leader development. *Journal of Leadership and Organizational Studies, 18,* 459–468.

Mayer, J. D., & Salovey, P. (1993). *The intelligence of emotional intelligence.* Elsevier.

McCormick, M. J., Tanguma, J., & Lopez–Forment, A. S. (2002). Extending self-efficacy theory to leadership: A review and empirical test. *Journal of Leadership Education, 1*(2), 1–15.

McEwen, M. K. (2003). New perspectives on identity development. In S. R. Komives & D. B. W. Jr. (Eds.), *Student services: A handbook for the profession* (pp. 203–233). Jossey-Bass.

Meichenbaum, D. (1985). Teaching thinking: A cognitive-behavioral perspective. In S. F. Chipman, J. W. Segal, & R. Glaser (Eds.), *Thinking and learning skills, Vol. 2: Research and open questions.* Lawrence Erlbaum.

Merriam, S. B., & Caffarella, R. S. (1999). *Learning in adulthood: A comprehensive guide.* Jossey-Bass.

Mulder, M., Gulikers, J., Wesselink, R., & Biemans, H. (2008). *The new competence concept in higher education: Error or enrichment?* Paper presented at American Educational Research Association annual meeting, New York, NY.

Mumford, M. D., Zaccaro, S. J., Connelly, M. S., & Marks, M. A. (2000). Leadership skills: Conclusions and future directions. *Leadership Quarterly, 11*(1), 155–170

Murphy, S. E., & Johnson, S. K. (2016). Leadership and leader developmental self-efficacy: Their role in enhancing leader development efforts. In R. J.

Reichard & S. E. Thompson (Eds.), *New Directions for Student Leadership: No. 149. Leader developmental readiness: Pursuit of leadership excellence* (pp. 73–84). Jossey-Bass.

Osteen, L., Guthrie, K. L., & Bertrand Jones, T. (2016). Leading to transgress: Critical considerations for transforming leadership learning. In K. L. Guthrie, T. Bertrand Jones, & L. Osteen (Eds.), *New Directions for Student Leadership: No. 152. Developing culturally relevant leadership learning* (pp. 95–106). Jossey-Bass.

Ospina, S. M., Foldy, E. G., El Hadidy, W. E., Dodge, J., Hofmann-Pinilla, A., & Su, C. (2012). Social change leadership as relational leadership. In M. Uhl-Bien & S. M. Ospina (Eds.), *Advancing relational leadership theory: A dialogue among perspectives* (pp. 255–302). Information Age Publishing.

Osteen, L., Mills, S., & Wiborg, E. R. (2020, August). [Lesson plan notes]. Center for Leadership and Social Change, Florida State University.

Owen, J. E. (2012). Using student development theories as conceptual frameworks in leadership education. In K. L. Guthrie & L. Osteen (Eds.), *New Directions for Student Services: No 140. Developing students' leadership capacity* (pp. 17–35). Jossey-Bass.

Owen, J. E., Hassell–Goodman, S., & Yamanaka, A. A. (2017). Culturally relevant leadership learning: Identity, capacity, and efficacy. *Journal of Leadership Studies, 11*(3), 48–54.

Patton, M. Q. (2002). *Qualitative research & evaluation methods* (3rd ed.). SAGE.

Preskill, S., & Brookfield, S. D. (2009). *Learning as a way of leading: Lessons from the struggle for social justice*. Jossey-Bass.

Reichard, R. J., & Walker, D. O. (2016). In pursuit: Mastering leadership through leader developmental readiness. In R. J. Reichard & S. E. Thompson (Eds.), *New Directions in Leadership Series: No. 149. Leader developmental readiness: Pursuit of leadership excellence* (pp. 15–26). Jossey-Bass.

Riggio, R. E., Ciulla, J. B., & Sorenson, G. J. (2003). Leadership education at the undergraduate level: A liberal arts approach to leadership development. In S. E. Murphy & R. E. Riggio (Eds.), *The future of leadership development* (pp. 223–236). Lawrence Erlbaum.

Rost, J. C. (1991). *Leadership for the twenty-first century*. Praeger.

Ruderman, M. N., & Ernst, C. (2004). Finding yourself: How social identity affects leadership. *Leadership in Action, 24*(3), 3–7.

Seemiller, C. (2013). *The student leadership competencies guidebook*. Jossey-Bass.

Seemiller, C., & Murray, T. (2013). The common language of leadership. *Journal of Leadership Studies, 7*(1), 33–45.

Sensoy, O., & DiAngelo, R. (2012). *Is everyone really equal? An introduction to key concepts in social justice education*. Teachers College.

Shankman, M. L., Allen, S. J., & Haber-Curran, P. (2015). *Emotionally intelligent leadership for students: Facilitation and activity guide*. Jossey-Bass.

Stryker, S., & Burke, P. J. (2000). The past, present, and future of an identity theory. *Social Psychology Quarterly, 63*(4), 284–297.

Tatum, B. D. (2017). *Why are all the black kids sitting together in the cafeteria?* (2nd ed.) Basic Books.

Turman, N. T., Alcozer Garcia, K. C., & Howes, S. (2018). Deepening attention to social location in building leader and leadership efficacy. In J. P. Dugan (Eds.), *New Directions for Student Leadership: No. 159. Integrating critical perspectives into leadership development* (pp. 65–76). Jossey-Bass.

Wagner, W. (2011). Considerations of student development in leadership. In S. R. Komives et al. (Eds.), *The handbook for student leadership development* (2nd ed., pp. 85–108). Jossey-Bass.

Warner, L. S., & Grint, K. (2006). American Indian ways of leading and knowing. *Leadership, 2*(2), 225–244.

Williams, T. O. (2016). Internalization of dominance and subordination: Barriers to creative and intellectual fullness. In K. L. Guthrie, T. Bertrand Jones, & L. Osteen (Eds.), *New Directions for Student Leadership: No. 152. Developing culturally relevant leadership learning* (pp. 87–94). Jossey-Bass.

Yosso, T. J. (2005). Whose culture has capital? A critical race theory discussion of community cultural wealth. *Race Ethnicity and Education, 8*(1), 69–91.

ABOUT THE AUTHORS

Kathy L. Guthrie (she/her/hers) grew up on a farm in Central Illinois, which was very influential in her identity as a leader. Kathy remembers learning about leadership while participating in her local 4-H club and various activities in high school like student council, class officer, show choir, captain of cheerleading squad, and running track. While an undergraduate student, she served as an orientation leader, on the campus programming board, and as a peer mentor for first year students. All these opportunities provided Kathy with experience in engaging in the leadership process. As an Associate Professor of Higher Education in the Department of Educational Leadership and Policy Studies at Florida State University, Kathy also serves as director of the Leadership Learning Research Center (LLRC), which coordinates the Undergraduate Certificate in Leadership Studies. Her research focuses on learning leadership and the outcomes and environment of leadership education. Prior to becoming a faculty member, Kathy served as a student affairs administrator for 10 years in various areas including campus activities, commuter services, community engagement, and leadership development. She has worked in higher education administrative and faculty roles for over 20 years and loves every minute of her chosen career path. Kathy enjoys spending time with her daughter and husband, where all three of them are affectionately known as Team Guthrie.

Cameron C. Beatty (he/him/his) is from Indianapolis, IN. Cameron's first memories of a leader are from his childhood when his mom would read children's books to him about Dr. Martin Luther King, Jr. Cameron came to realize that there were many civil rights leaders engaged in the leadership process who worked to address racial justice during the civil rights movement. Cameron's first memories of engaging in the leadership process were through is involvement in drill team at his church. He recognized through being a member of the drill team that collectively working towards a common goal can have a lasting impact on not only the group, but the individual contributing to the goals of the group. While an undergraduate student at Indiana University, Cameron was a student leader in his fraternity, Alpha Phi Alpha Fraternity, the National Pan-Hellenic Council, and the campus programming board. Cameron has worked in higher education for over 15 years and is currently an assistant professor in the Department of Educational Leadership and Policy Studies at Florida State University. He teaches courses in the undergraduate leadership studies program and the higher education graduate program, as well as conducts research with the Leadership Learning Research Center. Cameron's research focuses on socially just leadership education and the experiences of student leaders of Color navigating racial battle fatigue. In his free time, he enjoys long walks with his dog Zora.

Erica R. Wiborg (she/her/hers) was born and raised in Orlando, FL. As a child, Erica learned about leadership through sports and by observing her mom who worked as a Physical Education teacher/Athletic Director at her school. She often reflects on these observations—seeing her mom hold positional power and influence (using a whistle to organize a class or team), while balancing the gendered dynamics of being a woman leader in athletics. In college, Erica was involved in various organizations, including orientation, student activities, and fraternity/sorority life. After completing her master's degree in student affairs administration, Erica worked full-time coordinating college student development programs focused on leadership, social justice, identity, diversity, and community engagement. She took a few doctoral courses as a non-degree seeking student to develop her teaching skills and social justice knowledge, then decided to continue full-time coursework in the Higher Education PhD program at Florida State. She worked as a teaching assistant in the Leadership Learning Research Center where she taught in the undergraduate leadership studies program. Her courses focused on emotionally intelligent leadership, leadership theory, change, social justice, identity, and spirituality. Most recently, Erica worked as a research assistant, prior to graduating with her PhD. She studies college access and inequity in leadership learning; racism and whiteness in leadership; and college student leadership development.

www.ingramcontent.com/pod-product-compliance
Ingram Content Group UK Ltd.
Pitfield, Milton Keynes, MK11 3LW, UK
UKHW021920270325
456816UK00009B/99